Treating Anxiety

Using Cognitive Behavioral
Therapy Skills and Interventions

Books in This Series

Crisis Intervention for Community Behavioral Health Service Providers in Ohio

Overcoming Reluctance in Therapeutic Relationships

Psychotherapy for Families

Therapeutic Behavioral Services Using Interventions Based on Principles and Techniques of Cognitive Behavioral Therapy

Treating Attention Deficit Hyperactivity Disorder, Impulsivity, and Disruptive Behaviors in Children Using Behavioral Skill Building and Cognitive Behavioral Therapy Skills and Interventions

Treating Anxiety Using Cognitive Behavioral Therapy Skills and Interventions

Treating Depression Using Cognitive Behavioral Therapy Skills and Interventions

Treating Posttraumatic Stress Disorder Using Cognitive Behavioral Therapy Skills and Interventions

Treating Anxiety
Using Cognitive Behavioral Therapy Skills and Interventions

TREATMENT AND INTERVENTION MANUAL

Reinhild Boehme, LISW-S

Benjamin Kearney, PhD, *series editor*

THE INSTITUTE OF
FAMILY & COMMUNITY IMPACT

An OhioGuidestone Company
Berea, Ohio

Nothing contained in the manual is, or should be considered or used as, a substitute for medical advice, diagnosis, or treatment. The manual is not intended to replace, and does not replace, the specialized training and professional judgment of a health care or mental health care professional. Individuals should seek the advice of a physician or other health care provider with any questions regarding medications, personal health or medical conditions. This manual has been prepared as a tool to assist providers. In its efforts to provide information that is accurate and generally in accord with the standards of practice at the time of publication, the author has checked with sources believed to be reliable. However, in view of the possibility of human error or changes in behavioral, mental health, or medical sciences, neither the author, nor the editor and publisher, nor any other party who has been involved in the preparation or publication of this work warrants that the information contained herein is in every respect accurate or complete, and they are not responsible for any errors or omissions, or the results obtained from the use of such information. Further, the information presented in this manual does not constitute legal or financial advice or opinions. The ultimate responsibility for correct billing lies with the provider of the services. The reader should consult the current version of the relevant laws, regulations, and rulings.

The Institute of Family and Community Impact
An OhioGuidestone Company
www.OhioGuidestone.org

ISBN 978-1-7328190-7-8
Printed in the United States of America

Contents

Preface ix

Introduction 1

   Where to Start? 1

   Why Cognitive Behavioral Therapy? 2

CBT: The Essential Elements 3

   What Exactly Do We Mean When We Talk About the Cognitive
Component? 4

   But Where Do These Automatic Thoughts Come From? 4

   Where, Then, Do These Core Beliefs Come From? 5

   What About Behaviors? What Do We Mean When We Refer to the
Behavioral Component of the Cognitive Triad? 7

   What About the Emotional Component of the Cognitive Triad? 8

CBT in Action: How to Conceptualize a Case 11

   A Word About Suicide/Suicidal Ideation and Safety Planning 16

   A Word About Suicide Risk and Persistent Depressive Disorder 18

   Treatment Planning in CBT 19

   How to Build a CBT Treatment Plan 20

   What Is the Role of the Therapeutic Relationship in Cognitive
Behavioral Therapy? 23

   Being Attuned: Building Affect Regulation in the Therapeutic
Relationship 24

   What About Co-Regulation? 25

CBT Techniques and Structure 29

   Creating Structure 29

   Creating Structure When Discussing Course and Length of Treatment 31

   Essential CBT Techniques 32

Cognitive Behavioral Interventions for Anxiety 39

   Cognitive Interventions for Anxiety Disorders 41

      1. My Name is Failure 42

      2. Rotten Tomato Thoughts 45

      3. Finding a Place for Anxious Thoughts 48

      4. Visiting Anxious Thoughts 51

      5. Inviting In the Anxious Thought 54

6. Popping Anxious Bubbles 57

7. Disproving Anxious Thoughts 60

8. One More Page 63

9. Writing a Children's Story 65

10. Hearing Your Own Story 67

11. Train of Thoughts 69

12. It's Not the First Thought That Counts 72

13. No Food For Anxious Thoughts 75

14. Losing Your Marbles 80

15. Unwrapping It and Wrapping It Up 82

Behavioral Interventions for Anxiety Disorders 85

16. Skill Building: Breathe Through It 87

17. Behavior Baseline 89

18. Skill Building: Opening the Senses, Opening the Mind 91

19. Skill Building: Move Through It 93

20. Skill Building: Change the Scenery 95

21. Leaning into Discomfort 97

22. Facing Anxiety: Beginning Exposure 100

23. Facing Anxiety: Stepping Up Exposure 103

24. Facing Anxiety: Stepping to the Top 106

25. Working with Failure 108

26. When Anxiety Returns 111

27. Exposure: Jumping for Joy 114

28. Expanding the Window of Tolerance 117

29. Walking Out the Door 122

30. Ending Treatment 125

Interventions Working with the Emotional Component of the Triad 127

31. The Flood 128

32. Going with the Flow 130

33. Being Well Prepared for the Flood of Anxious Thoughts
Versus Frantic Preparation 132

34. The Observer 135

35. The Examiner 137

36. From Observation to Action 140

37. Anxious Feelings: Exposure 101 142

38. Anxious Feelings: Stepping Up Exposure 145

39. Exposure to Anxious Feelings: Stepping to the Top 149

40. Still Feeling Anxious: Managing the Anxious Feelings
That Are Left 153

Working with Phobias. 155

  Jared's Phobia in Context. 156

  Skill Building Interventions 159

    41. Breathe Through It 160

    42. Skill Building: Opening the Senses, Opening the Mind 162

    43. Skill Building: Move Through It 164

    44. Skill Building: Change the Scenery 166

    45. Skill Building: Firmly Grounded 168

  Exposure Interventions 171

    46. Facing Anxiety: Beginning Exposure 172

    47. Facing Anxiety: Stepping Up Exposure 175

    48. Facing Anxiety: Stepping to the Top 178

    49. Working with Failure 180

Appendix: Selected Figures 185

References 221

Preface

For mental health professionals, building trusting relationships with clients and knowing which interventions will most benefit them are challenging enough. Helping clients who are also dealing at the same time with chronic conditions such as poverty, violence, and addiction can seem overwhelming. That's especially true for behavioral health service providers who have limited experience. That's why we at OhioGuidestone have developed this series of clinical manuals to help professionals develop their skills while providing effective treatment.

OhioGuidestone, the largest community behavioral health organization in Ohio, regularly trains new therapists and other behavioral health interventionists to work with clients who face severe, therapy-interfering challenges. We've brought that experience to these manuals.

In this era of managed care oversight, tight funding, and pressure to deliver evidence-based or informed care, it is essential for new therapists to get up to speed on best practices quickly. It is also essential for experienced clinicians to be well provided with effective and varied treatment plans. The manuals in this series provide step-by-step guidance on evidence-based and informed treatment modalities and interventions that can be used by both licensed and unlicensed mental health professionals—as well as by their supervisors for training purposes.

Seasoned mental health professionals will find the resources offered in these manuals useful for developing a renewed focus on evidence- and research-based interventions. At OhioGuidestone, our interventions are grounded in cognitive behavioral science and also shaped by the relational and attachment scientific advances that continue to inform the behavioral health field (especially the interpersonal neurobiology work published by W. W. Norton & Company). We understand the demands of serving client populations experiencing trauma and toxic stress. Our interventions are designed not to address discrete diagnoses (clients often have more than one) but rather the symptoms that are related to them. The series addresses a wide range of issues, such as depression, anxiety, ADHD, PTSD, and even reluctance to engage in therapy, and it provides interventions for children and adults.

We cannot "fix" our clients. But we can guide them along clear paths toward developing the skills they need to navigate the challenges they face, in their thoughts and in their lives. It's our sincere hope that the books in this series will help better prepare more mental health professionals to do just that.

— Benjamin Kearney, PhD, series editor

If you purchased this manual and want to make copies of interventions to help your clients, please do so. However, please do not share copies with other professionals but encourage them to buy manuals for themselves. This will help us continue to add to and update this series, to better equip all helpers who make a difference.

Introduction

This manual is for licensed mental health providers who provide psychotherapy and related services.

Treating anxious clients can feel like a tall order. It is not unusual for clients to show up for treatment after they have suffered from symptoms for years. Their lives may have already shrunk in many ways. Perhaps they are so anxious they have stopped participating in social activities. Perhaps their anxiety is manifested in angry outbursts and mistaken for an anger-management problem. It may seem to them that their anxiety is unmanageable. In an attempt to feel less anxious, your clients may continue to eliminate activities and people from their lives, yet this only temporarily relieves the anxiety.

This manual will help you and your clients think differently about anxiety and its symptoms. Your client will learn to rationally examine anxious thoughts and feelings using evidence. You will then work with your client on adjusting the way she thinks, feels, and acts to better match the realities of life as it is, as opposed to life as viewed through the lens of anxious thoughts and feelings.

Additionally, you will learn to view anxiety through the lens of neurobiology. Anxiety, at its core, is physical. It's not just a psychological phenomenon, but rather a full body, brain, and mind experience.

This manual will not specifically address the treatment of posttraumatic stress disorder due to its different etiology. While posttraumatic stress disorder is an anxiety disorder, the presence of a clear precipitating traumatic event calls for a specific approach, which will be outlined in *Treating Posttraumatic Stress Disorder*.

Where to Start?

If you would like a very brief and concise introduction to cognitive behavioral therapy (CBT) for Anxiety, read *Psychotherapy Essentials to Go: Cognitive Behavioral Therapy for Anxiety* by Mark Fefergrad and Ari Zaretsky. This book includes a laminated pull-out practice reminder card as well as a DVD with practice examples, including client role play.

If you would like a more in-depth overview of the theoretical foundations of CBT, as well as step-by-step practice guidelines integrated with case examples and theoretical musings, you may want to read the following books: *Evidence-Based Practice of Cognitive Behavioral Therapy* by Deborah Dobson and Keith S. Dobson, and *Doing CBT: A Comprehensive Guide to Working with Behaviors, Thoughts, and Emotions* by David F. Tolin.

If you are looking for a book outlining how to recognize and treat comorbidity in anxious clients, you may want to read *Tough-to-Treat Anxiety: Hidden Problems and Effective Solutions for your Clients* by Margaret Wehrenberg.

While the last book is not rooted in the cognitive behavioral therapy philosophy, it will be helpful when something gets in the way of treating an anxiety disorder, such as a comorbid autism spectrum disorder of attention deficit disorder.

Why Cognitive Behavioral Therapy?

There are many validated reasons for using cognitive behavioral therapy (CBT) for the treatment of anxiety.

Conceptually, CBT offers a structured approach to treatment that creates a "counterweight" to the chaos anxiety can cause. When there seems no way out and change seems impossible, CBT always offers a next step because it insists on clear goals, a structure for each session, and a structure for the course of treatment.

Equally important is the fact that CBT is identified as evidence-based and has strong research support. The Society for Clinical Psychology (2016) identifies behavior therapy and cognitive therapy as having strong research support for the treatment of anxiety, specifically generalized anxiety disorder, panic disorder, and social anxiety disorder.

The *Practitioners Guide to Evidence-Based Psychotherapy* (Fisher & O'Donohue, 2006) notes that CBT is evidence-based and empirically strongly supported for the treatment of generalized anxiety disorder (p. 305), panic disorder (p. 496), and social anxiety disorder (p. 671). Systematic desensitization coupled with psychoeducation and cognitive restructuring (all components of cognitive behavioral therapy) is identified as empirically supported for the treatment of specific phobias (p. 647).

Research and evidence support that cognitive behavioral therapy is an effective treatment for various anxiety disorders. Does this mean that it is right for your client?

Because CBT is evidence-based and empirically supported, it must be offered to your client. You should explain that CBT is a well-researched treatment. You should also explain that all treatment, including CBT, will be tailored to fit the needs of the client. Using CBT does not mean disregarding client opinions, needs, and preferences. On the contrary, it means working with the client within the CBT framework.

What if your client is a child or struggles with complex ideas and thoughts?

CBT is not dependent on using complex models and language. CBT language can easily be adapted to fit a child's (or adult's) developmental level. The following book is a good example of this: *CBT Strategies for Anxious and Depressed Children and Adolescents* by Eduardo L. Bunge, Javier Mandil, Andrés J. Consoli and Martin Gomar.

Additionally, you may want to begin working on the behavioral component of the cognitive triad (see below) for clients who are less inclined to conceptualize things. Beginning with this is consistent with the framework and philosophy of CBT.

CBT: The Essential Elements

Cognitive behavioral therapy, or CBT, focuses on addressing three elements: Thoughts (also known as cognitions), feelings (also known as emotions), and behaviors (actions). Note that in CBT, this is called the *cognitive triad*. Why is it called the cognitive triad (not the feelings or emotional triad)? Ultimately, CBT holds that all kinds of problems, be they behavioral or emotional problems, are rooted in unrealistic and faulty thinking. Hence, unrealistic and faulty thinking must be identified and corrected.

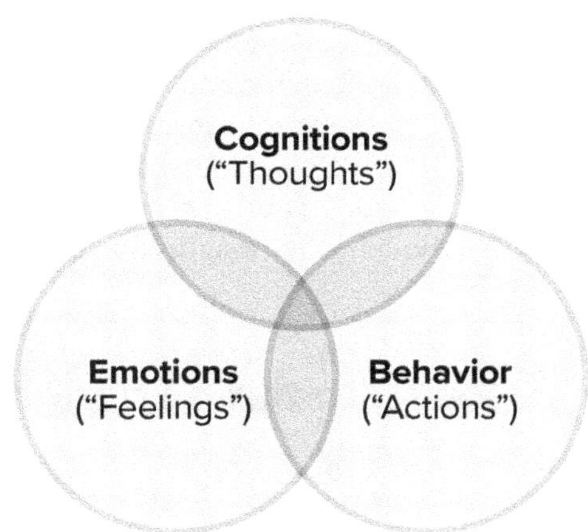

Figure 1

This conceptualization contains three components:

- the emotional component,

- the behavioral component, and

- the cognitive component.

- These three interact with each other. Thoughts, especially automatic thoughts (thoughts that just "happen"; Tolin [2016, p. 57] calls them "interpretations" because they usually interpret what is happening in some unpleasant way), impact behaviors and emotions. But behaviors also impact emotions and cognitions.

What Exactly Do We Mean When We Talk About the Cognitive Component?

Simply put: What and how we think impacts how we feel and what we do. But do we always know what we are thinking? Beck et al. (1979) observed "the depressed person's tendency to interpret his ongoing experiences in a negative way" (p. 11). He used the metaphor of an intercom to bring this internal chatter into the therapeutic conversation. Beck named this uninvited and ever-present chatter "automatic thoughts." These are the thoughts we did not ask for and are often only somewhat aware of.

Here are some examples of automatic thoughts:

- I always mess everything up.
- She hates me.
- I am going to fail this one.

Notice that automatic thoughts are judgmental in nature. They don't often compliment us. If they do, they are not problematic and seldom a topic in treatment. It would be a good idea, however, to track the transformation from negative automatic thoughts to more realistic thoughts during the course of treatment.

If your client is a child, you may want to find another name for automatic thoughts. You could try: "buggy thoughts" = thoughts that bug me.

But Where Do These Automatic Thoughts Come From?

In CBT, basic negative views of self, others, and the world are called *core beliefs* or *schemas*. We may hold these beliefs without being aware of them. They drive how we think about ourselves consciously and unconsciously (internal chatter), each other, and the world. Automatic thoughts are rooted in core beliefs. For the most part, we are not aware of the core beliefs we hold.

Here are some examples of core beliefs:

- I am unworthy.
- I am a failure.
- I am unlovable.

These, of course, are examples of unhealthy core beliefs. Here are some examples of healthy core beliefs:

- I am worthy.
- I am capable.
- I am lovable.

Where, Then, Do These Core Beliefs Come From?

In CBT this is an interesting question, because CBT insists on a focus on the here and now. We may never know where specifically our core beliefs come from. Or we may know. But we cannot deconstruct them by simply knowing who to blame for our core negative beliefs. Yes, perhaps a parent instilled a sense of worthlessness that led to a core belief of unworthiness. But CBT is what Tolin (2016) calls "present oriented" (p. 8). It is not that CBT discredits what has happened to a client or disregards the emotional pain that the past may have caused him or her. Rather CBT insists that the client move into the here and now. The question to our client then becomes:

- *What do you think/believe about what happened to you?*

- *Are there other, more realistic and accurate ways of thinking about the past/the impact of the past?*

In other words, faulty core beliefs and negative automatic thoughts can be corrected here and now. In an interesting way, CBT has clarity about harmful core beliefs such as: "I am unlovable." These beliefs are simply not true because they are not evidence-based.

Here is an example of what correcting faulty thinking about past hurt might look like.

- Your client was neglected by her parents and emotionally and sexually abused. She holds the core belief that she is "ruined for life." Her automatic thoughts about the past tell her that she is "dirty" and that no one would want her. Because of these thoughts she is anxious about relationships as she believes all of her relationships will ultimately fail.

- CBT would acknowledge the hurt but move towards correcting those faulty automatic thoughts using evidence from the here and now.

CBT insists that we rationally tackle faulty core beliefs *now,* that the core belief must be examined using empirical methods (evidence) and then adjusted to a more realistic core belief. More adaptive and realistic core beliefs then lead to more adaptive and realistic thoughts that correct negative automatic thoughts. More realistic thoughts about self, other, and the world lead to behaviors that are a better fit for reality and hence produce a better outcome.

The following diagram shows how thoughts (cognitions) are viewed in CBT:

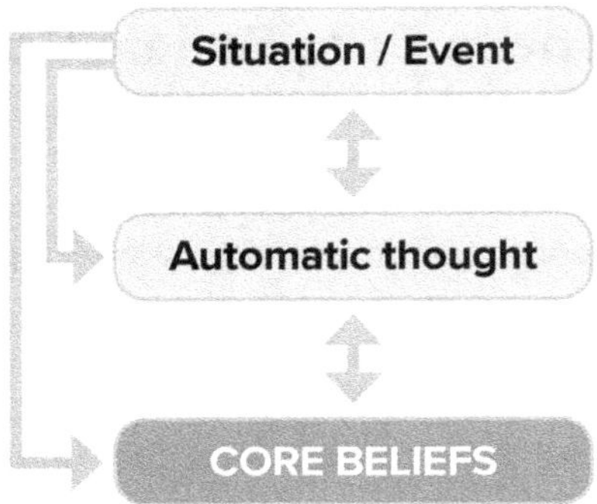

Figure 2: Note that core beliefs are much harder to identify than automatic thoughts (AT's). AT's just appear, we do not have to ask for them. Because they appear so often, they are easier to bring into conscious awareness.

An event/situation triggers a core belief. The core belief results in negative automatic thoughts. These negative automatic thoughts lead to behaviors that are not a good "fit" for the situation because they are faulty interpretations of what is actually going on.

Here is an example of what this may look like:

Jason feels anxious about his new relationship. Today he is having an argument with his partner. As soon as the disagreement begins, he hears himself saying to himself: "Stupid, I am so stupid."

This automatic thought is rooted in Jason's core belief that he is unworthy. He developed this core belief as a young child due to ongoing emotional neglect.

Jason is overwhelmed by both anxiety and sadness (the emotional component of the cognitive triad) and lashes out at his partner, then leaves to never return (the behavioral component of the triad).

What went wrong?

Jason did not assess the situation accurately. He is clearly not "stupid" (finished high school, works as a mechanic), but he does have a core belief that he is stupid and unlovable (clearly also not true as he is currently in a loving relationship). He reacts emotionally to his negative automatic thoughts, and his actions are based on the intense emotions of anxiety and anger.

The key in Jason's treatment is to get him away from faulty interpretations into more accurate interpretations of what is truly happening right now. Here is what that might look like:

Jason is having an argument with his partner. They disagree, and it is difficult for him to accept that they are in disagreement. This initially makes Jason anxious because it triggers an automatic thought that he is stupid and a core belief that he is unworthy. This in turn triggers the anxious behavior of leaving (with the thought of never returning).

Jason comes to understand that disagreements are a normal part of any relationship. He recognizes his anxiety about having a disagreement, but he moves past this and tries to work out a compromise with his partner. When the couple reach a compromise he feels validated, competent, and less anxious.

What About Behaviors? What Do We Mean When We Refer to the Behavioral Component of the Cognitive Triad?

Inaccurate core beliefs lead to inaccurate automatic thoughts about a situation. These automatic, negative, and rapid-fire thoughts lead to behavioral responses that are based on a faulty assessment of the situation. If I assume that things will go wrong no matter what I do, my assessment of the future will be a negative one. If my assessment of the future is that is it precarious, taking action becomes anxiety provoking. I may ask myself: What if I make the wrong decision? Because of this anxiety, I may struggle with making any decision, even smaller ones. How should I act, how can I act, when my actions can have far-reaching consequences? Anxiety can be expressed as inaction or as frantic action. Anxiety may tell your client that nothing she does will work out. As a consequence she may simply "freeze" and do nothing. Alternatively, she may frantically try one ineffective approach after another. Both approaches are not a good "fit" for reality and lead to more negative automatic anxious thoughts.

Note that a main behavioral component of anxiety can be inaction and indecisiveness. This behavioral component can easily "flip" into aggression (a rebellion against anxious feelings). It is important to understand that aggression can be and often is an expression of anxiety, especially in children.

Behaviors based on a faulty interpretation of self, others, and the world maintain anxiety. In order to address anxiety, behaviors have to change. In CBT this is called *behavioral activation.* When using behavioral activation we help our clients realize that "doing better in order to feel better" (Tolin, 2016, p. 39) can work.

The following diagram shows how behavioral components relate to the cognitive components of anxiety:

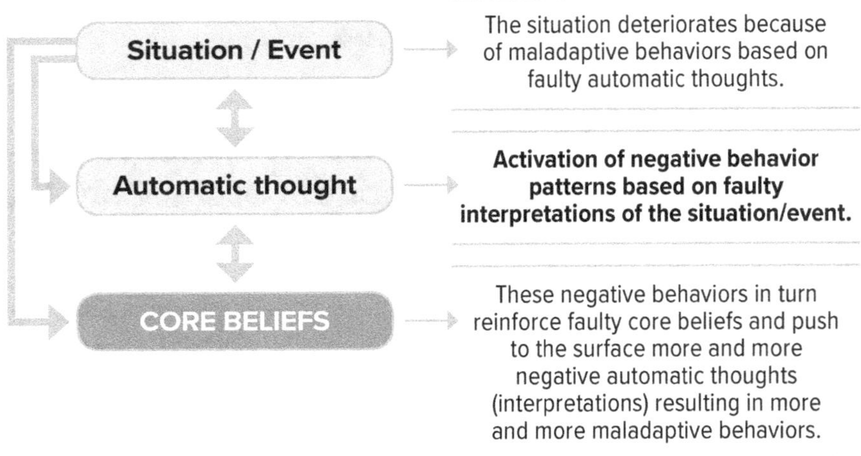

Figure 3

What About the Emotional Component of the Cognitive Triad?

What are emotions, really? Why do we have them? Do they serve a basic purpose?

Tolin (2016) acknowledges that there are basic human emotions that are biologically based. They have a function. Fear, for example, evolutionarily speaking, is meant to keep us alive. So is love. He differentiates between "physiological sensations" (p. 81) and "subjective emotional states." In other words: There are basic "emotions" that we need. They keep us alive.

In other words, the physiological components of anxiety are built in us to keep us alive. These are things like an increased heart rate and the release of stress hormones. These things get us going and are designed to ensure survival. Vigilance is useful for survival when there is a real chance that we may be attacked by a wild animal. In that case, the ability to instantly mobilize for fight or flight is also critical. Modern human beings, however, are often stuck in the evolutionarily prescribed response (fight/flight) that is no longer useful. When we are anxious it feels like we are under attack by a tiger even if there is no tiger.

When the physiological components of anxiety trigger a psychological state and the psychological state is disconnected from reality (because there is not real danger), anxiety is born. Beck et al. (1976, p. 151) describes the basic cognitive error leading to increased anxiety: If I feel anxious (and perhaps this is simply triggered by a bodily sensation), I may think and believe (on the basis of feeling anxious) that there is danger. I then feel even more anxious. The reaction becomes problematic if there is no actual danger.

Feelings of anxiety can be triggered by loneliness. Neurobiologically we are not designed to be alone. We are designed to be a part of a group that protects us and helps us regulate feelings. Therefore, when we feel fundamentally alone (even when we are not actually alone), anxiety can be triggered.

Emotions are impacted by physiological states.

If, for example, I fear my racing heart, I may avoid anything that raises my heart rate and feel anxious about my perceived inability to be physically active. The feeling of fear and the inaccurate assessment of reality (assuming that nothing is really medically wrong) is pushing me into inactivity, which in turn makes me feel like a failure (automatic thought leading to feelings of failure). Physical activity, however, may be needed to regulate anxiety. So my anxiety may not decrease because I am not physically active.

Emotions, behaviors, automatic thoughts (and ultimately core beliefs), and the body are intimately connected, always interacting with each other. Emotions can be incredibly adaptive when they move us into the right kind of action.

Here is an example:

You may feel anxious because you have not completed a project that is due tomorrow. In this case, anxiety functions like a big red blinking light, telling you to take action. And if you take action and complete the project, your anxiety will likely decrease. But if you wait and delay taking action, you may feel more anxious. You may become so anxious that you feel that you can't take action because your anxiety has incapacitated you and sent you into the "freeze" part of the fight/flight/freeze response.

So here is how the emotional components of anxiety relate to the behavioral and cognitive components:

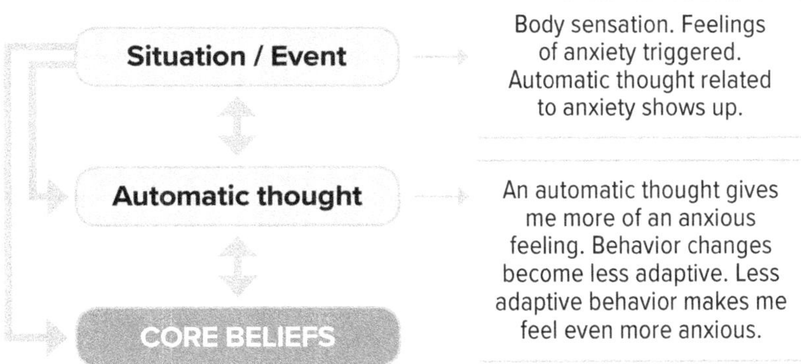

Figure 4

CBT in Action: How to Conceptualize a Case

CBT offers a clear path to treatment in that it insists that after a thorough assessment you must develop a clear *case formulation* (Dobson & Dobson, 2017). Tolin (2016) calls this a "meaty conceptualization" of your case (p. 94). In other words: We must create a hypothesis of what all is creating and maintaining the problem.

Once you have completed your case conceptualization you are ready to identify your intervention targets. In other words: You are ready to create a treatment plan.

But before you do so, you must put your case conceptualization on paper. Where does it go?

Your case conceptualization belongs in the **Clinical Summary Section of the Diagnostic Evaluation in Evolv**. When you write your Clinical Summary, be sure to include the behavioral, emotional, and cognitive elements that create and maintain your client's problems. Also, specifically name what problems you want to target for your client. The problems you have identified become the basis of your treatment plan.

Let's walk through a case:

Case Vignette: Sheney

Sheney is a 25-year-old African American mother of two young children ages one and three. She was recently laid off from her position as a manager at a local fast food restaurant and has been feeling anxious ever since. She constantly worries about her family's future and about having to move "back to the projects" because without a job she will not be able to pay the rent for her two-bedroom apartment much longer.

Every time the mail arrives, Sheney worries so much that she does not open it. She just tosses it in a pile in the corner. Sheney's worry has incapacitated her, and she no longer goes out to look for work. She feels that the neighbors are staring at her and is afraid that they know what is happening. Lately, Sheney has been pacing in the apartment. She tries to play with her children but is so worried about the future that she has a hard time looking at them. She is now convinced that it will be just a matter of time before her children will be taken from her.

Additionally, Sheney is worried about her health as she constantly feels her heart racing. At night she listens to her heartbeat and worries when it is not regular. She also often checks to make sure that both of her children are breathing. Hence, she does not get much sleep.

When she feels overwhelmed Sheney eats whatever she can find in the house—most often a bag of chips or leftover French fries.

Sheney does not own a car, and the convenience store around the corner only sells packaged food.

Sheney's case is not an uncommon one. Our clients are often faced with multiple barriers, many of which are beyond their control. Let's call them *therapy interfering conditions (TICs)*. Here are some examples of therapy interfering conditions:

- poverty
- lack of education
- incarceration of a family member
- disability
- racism
- sexism

While our clients are faced with these conditions (they did not choose them), they are forced to deal with them. There is ample evidence that conditions of toxic stress, especially in childhood, can contribute to the development of physical and mental illness. You can find more information about the impact of toxic stress and trauma from Aces Too High at www.acestoohigh.com.

How can CBT be helpful when there are therapy interfering conditions present?

- CBT can help correct automatic thoughts of self-blame about conditions beyond the client's control.

- CBT can help the client focus on taking action. Moving into action can take many forms, one of them being advocating for social justice.

- CBT can help the client take action for herself/himself, moving from helplessness to a sense of self-efficacy (working in the behavioral part of the cognitive triad).

Community Mental Health Practice Alert

What about the conditions many of our clients live in? What about poverty?

Sheney lives in poverty as many of our clients do. She has few external resources. She does not have a car. She does not have savings. Her support system is crumbling. Access to healthy foods is limited.

Your case conceptualization must incorporate the conditions Sheney lives in. They have shaped her way of thinking and being – and her specific anxious responses.

Incorporating conditions of toxic stress into the case conceptualization models for Sheney that not everything is her fault. Incorporating conditions of toxic stress also incorporates a behavioral component into her treatment. When Sheney is ready to do so, she may want to take value-based action and develop or increase her advocacy for herself and others living in poverty.

In other words: Sheney would learn to take action again. Taking action to create change is a behavior we would want to increase through the use of CBT. Keep in mind that this behavior will have to be modeled and taught.

In other words: Anxiously avoiding action in an inherent component of anxiety is a symptom that can be treated and changed. Anxiously jumping from one ineffective course of action to another is another anxiety symptom that can be treated.

A Case Conceptualization for Sheney:

Sheney: Assessment and Case Conceptualization/ Problem Identification

Use the Diagnostic Evaluation (DE) Part 1 and Part 2. Include information about Sheney's socioeconomic status in the DE.

Here is what your Clinical Summary (case conceptualization) may look like:

Sheney's anxious thoughts, feelings, and behaviors were initially triggered by the loss of her job.

She is feeling anxious about the future, and this anxiety is now impacting the way she thinks and acts. Specifically, Sheney is struggling with anxious automatic thoughts and taking action.

Sheney has become anxious about her body and about her children as evidenced by her increased focus on listening to her own heartbeat and listening to her children's breathing at night.

Furthermore, Sheney is impacted by a lack of external resources as well as a struggle to access the resources that are available. This, in turn, reinforces her anxiousness as she feels that there is just no way out of the situation.

Sheney's cognitive processes are focused on anxious rumination and shame, which are reinforced daily by negative self-talk (automatic thoughts) and inactivity. Additionally, Sheney blames herself for eating poorly.

Because her symptoms began only recently after the onset of a clearly identifiable stressor, Sheney meets criteria for adjustment disorder with anxiety.

Problems:

1. Cognitive: Attention focused on anxious thoughts, ruminates, automatic thoughts, self-blame
2. Behavioral: Inaction based on constant worry, lack of interaction with her children, anxious body focus (self and children)
3. Emotional: Anxious shame and self-blame

Note that the problem list does not encompass all of Sheney's problems, but rather focuses on what is most important. We would want to focus on the behavioral components of treatment first: Better sleep, better nutrition, appropriate medical care, and improved stability are likely to impact Sheney's symptoms.

You have completed your case conceptualization. This is a good time to check with your client.

Ask:

- *Did I get this right?*
- *Is there anything I left out?*
- *Is there anything I need to add?*

Make sure that you are working collaboratively with your client on identifying problems and treatment goals. While CBT can be more directive than other forms of therapy, collaboration ensures that a therapeutic alliance and a "joint ownership" are built (Dobson and Dobson, 2017, p. 53). A solid therapeutic alliance, client and therapist ownership of the case formulation, problem identification, and treatment planning are the basis for treatment success.

What can happen if you don't work collaboratively?

If you don't work collaboratively, treatment success is jeopardized from the start. You may think that *you* understand your client's basic problems. You may have a great case conceptualization in your mind, and you may even be correct in the way you conceptualize a case. However, if your client disagrees with you, she may never fully participate in treatment. Any goals you may have established may be partially irrelevant to her; hence, she may not be committed to the course of treatment you are thinking about, and treatment success becomes questionable.

How can you ensure that you are working collaboratively with your client?

- Ask frequently: Did I get this right? Is there anything you want to add? What part of what I am saying does not sit right with you?

- If your client is not ready for the kind of change you have in mind, go back to basics. Ask the miracle question: If you had one wish and it would come true tomorrow morning, what would your wish be? (Jong & Berg, 2013).

- Build collaboration based on that wish. If you are working with a child (or a very materialistic adult), you may have to explore the differences between material-istic things your client wants versus the life he or she wants.

- Acknowledge reluctance and ambivalence before and while you encourage your client to move into change processes. Voice understanding that change is hard.

- Understand that collaboration and trust are built and that it is your responsibil-ity to create their foundation. In other words, you will have to model collabora-tion and trust.

Assessment of what specifically impacts your client and causes anxious symp-toms should encompass all three aspects of CBT: thoughts, feelings, and behaviors. Assessment should be collaborative and structured. Assessment should utilize valid standardized measures and should lead to a case formulation laid out in the clinical summary of the diagnostic evaluation in Evolv. The clinical summary must conclude with an identification of problems (in order of importance).

Once problems have been identified collaboratively, the treatment plan can be completed.

Here is a visual representation of the assessment process:

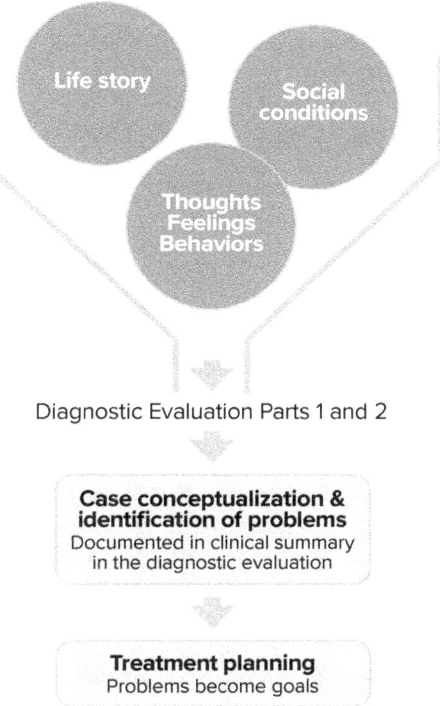

Figure 5

A Word About Suicide/Suicidal Ideation and Safety Planning

If your client discloses thoughts of suicide, complete a formalized suicide risk assessment. Do so in a caring and compassionate manner, stating that you are asking your client these questions because you want her to be well. Document completion of a formal suicide risk assessment in your case notes, and ensure that the suicide risk assessment is scanned into the client's electronic record.

Once you have completed the formalized suicide risk assessment, you will need to complete a safety plan. **Any safety concerns about a client must also be reported and discussed with your supervisor on the day that they occur.**

What is the function of a safety plan? Tolin (2016) rightfully points out that safety planning in no way guarantees that your client will not harm herself. What a safety plan does, however, is denote to both you and the client the importance of the matter and specifically the importance of taking action.

By collaboratively creating a safety plan with your client, you are:

- expressing genuine concern and compassion for your client. You are expressing that you value her as a human being, and you want her to stay alive so she can create "a life worth living" (Dimeff & Linehan, 2001, p. 2); and

- modeling immediately the importance of taking (positive and life affirming) action. Sometimes anxious feelings become so intense, so unbearable, that they "flip" into depressive feelings. If this happens, pay close attention to your client's level of depression and hopelessness by asking clear questions about suicidal thoughts and behaviors.

What Should Be Included in a Safety Plan?

Use the OGS Safety Planning Form to create your safety plan. This form will identify:

- concerning thoughts,

- concerning behaviors,

- things the client can do (behavioral activation to shift attention),

- people the client can talk to (behavioral activation aimed at changing attentional focus to supportive and caring relationships), and

- triggers and their removal from the environment. If medications are a trigger, they should be secured. No person with suicidal thoughts should have access to firearms in the home. Even if they are locked away, the risk of gaining access is there. A plan should be made to temporarily remove any firearms from the home.

Can a Safety Plan Guarantee the Safety of Your Client?

A safety plan cannot guarantee the safety of your client. It does, however, indicate that you and your client have adequately addressed the issue of suicidal thoughts and behaviors and that you, the clinician, have actively taken all appropriate steps to help your client stay safe and alive.

What About Children?

When creating a safety plan with a child, the parent must always be involved. If a child discloses a safety issue and the parent is not present, you must contact the parent immediately (and notify your supervisor). A meeting with the parent or guardian must be scheduled on the same day to create a safety plan. Remember, safety planning is a collaborative process. A meaningful safety plan involves addressing both the concerns of the parent and the concerns of the child.

What Will Not Work

- Meeting with the client and parent with a ready-made safety plan that does not take into account the specific family circumstances.

- Creating a vague safety plan, including statements such as "will call a friend" or "parent will put away all medications."

- Things that are impossible, such as "parent will supervise client at all times" when the parent works full time.

What Will Work

- Being compassionate and inquisitive about the client's and family's specific circumstances. Learn as much as you can to collaboratively create a workable safety plan.

- Being specific. Outline specifically where the client will go, who the client can call (include phone numbers), and what the client will do. An example of this would be: "Client will build a Lego Tower in the kitchen while guardian . . ."

- Things that are possible, such as: "Parent will ensure appropriate supervision of client. Aunt . . . will play Legos with client/go for a walk with client."

What If Nothing Works?

Sometimes nothing seems to work. When this is the case, it is important to consider the following factors:

- Is there anything reinforcing the client's need to be hospitalized? In other words, will the client receive more attention and perhaps compassion if she is so ill that she requires hospitalization? Does the client actually need more attention? If so, how can your client receive more attention? Is a partial hospitalization program needed? Some form of respite care? Keep in mind that your client may express an actual need. This is not manipulation on the client's part. She may not be able to tell you (yet) what she needs. This, in itself, is a clinical issue that requires attention.

- If your client is a child: Is the parent simply exhausted from caring for a mentally ill child? Is a more intensive level of services needed? Is respite needed? Does the parent need her own services?

- Is the client/family in a very dysregulated state? Can you assist with helping calm emotions? Can you instill hope that things will get better?

Sometimes hospitalization is needed to stabilize a client. This does not mean that you or the client missed something. It does mean that a better plan is needed. It is important to begin with planning for discharge right away. What will be different? What can you do? What can your client do? How can the environment change?

A Word About Suicide Risk and Persistent Depressive Disorder

What is a Persistent Depressive Disorder?

This includes those of your clients who have suffered from persistent low mood for at least two years (for children the time frame is one year) with or without any symptoms of a major depressive episode.

In the fifth edition of the *Diagnostic and Statistical Manual of Mental Disorders* (DSM-5; 2013) this combination of symptoms is called persistent depressive disorder (300.4).

What About Suicide Risk and Persistent Depressive Disorder?

If your client has suffered from persistent low mood and is now experiencing additional symptoms of a major depression (including hopelessness), assess for suicide risk. Your client may feel that the additional heavy weight of major depression is just too much for her to handle. This can put her at a higher risk for suicidal thoughts and behaviors.

In other words: When your client has a persistent depressive disorder that has always included or now does include symptoms of a major depression, you must assess for suicide risk.

Treatment Planning in CBT

Safety always comes first. If there are client behaviors such as suicidal gestures or actions or severe self-harm (that may not be intended to but could result in death), these need to be addressed first. There are many ways in which CBT responds to suicidal behaviors. Here are some of them:

- making the environment safe by identifying and removing triggers

- changing client behavioral responses to triggers

- increasing skills to manage triggers and resulting emotional states (skill building)

- examining and changing automatic thoughts leading to suicidal behaviors

Is it necessary to address all three elements of the cognitive triad in the treatment plan? What about behavioral interventions for those who struggle with thinking things through (a factor very much inherent in anxiety)?

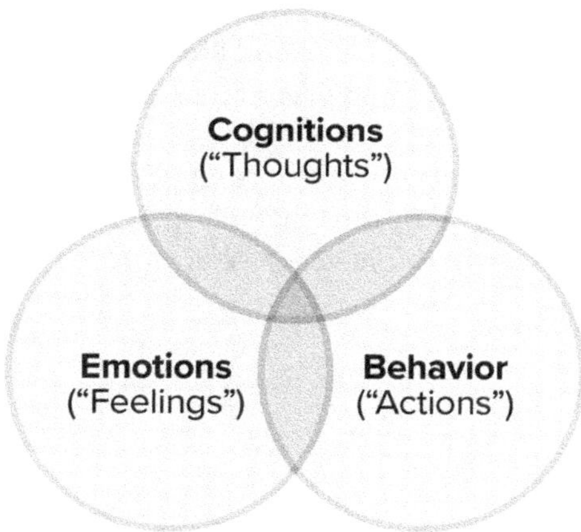

Figure 6: The cognitive triad

It is not necessary to address all three elements of the cognitive triad equally and right away. In fact, Tolin (2016), referring to behavioral interventions, recommends that "you should strongly consider using these strategies as the 'main course' in your CBT" (p. 161).

Why start with behavioral interventions?

Generally speaking, interventions targeting behaviors may be more accessible to clients. In addition, when it comes to the treatment of anxiety, we are looking to move the client into thoughtful and calm and realistic action—away from frozen inaction or frantic ineffective action.

In other words, targeting behavioral symptoms may be the most accessible "door" to treating anxiety. When your client is taking frantic action based on her anxious thoughts and feelings, she is likely to be ineffective in managing her life. If that can be changed and your client can learn to take calm and realistic action, she is likely to develop a greater sense of control over life. This sense of control will decrease her anxious thoughts and feelings.

Community Mental Health Practice Alert

Our clients often struggle with basic skills for many reasons. Remember those therapy interfering conditions?

Lack of resources related to poverty in itself can make our clients anxious. It makes sense that our clients are anxious when they have to think about losing their housing or food stamps.

Therapy interfering conditions can lead to skill deficits in people who are otherwise competent. Poverty may lead to an educational impairment. It is difficult to learn when you are hungry or worried about housing. It is difficult to learn when you have to move a lot. If you grew up in an old house and you have been exposed to lead, learning can become a real challenge.

While our clients may have skill deficits, this does not mean that they are incapable of learning. It is not a good idea to underestimate our clients' ability to learn, grow, and overcome.

Psychoeducation and behavioral interventions can be very empowering for our clients. The experience of competence is a very powerful experience that can lead to further changes in thinking, feeling, and behavior—just the kind of ripple effect we are looking for.

How to Build a CBT Treatment Plan

1. Address safety issues first. This includes creating a safety plan right away if one is needed. If you are unsure whether one is needed, consult with your supervisor.
2. Start with behavioral interventions, such as creating a schedule of activities, building real world skills, building relationships, becoming active—all of this with the goal of increasing your client's sense of control over her life.
3. Address cognitive elements such as automatic thoughts as they occur. Help your client change negative automatic self-talk. If your client has had some success using behavioral interventions, this will be a natural step as you now have evidence that your client is competent and that things can go well. Help your client use the evidence!
4. Address faulty thinking such as, "Things need to go well all the time."
5. Be on the lookout for core beliefs and use Socratic questioning to address faulty core beliefs.

What are Socratic questions?

Tolin (2016, p. 159) defines Socratic questions as "a way of helping the client arrive at a conclusion by asking carefully worded questions."

Here are some examples of Socratic questions:

- What does this mean to you?
- How did you come to think about the event this way?
- Is there another possible way of thinking about this event?
- How do you know that what you are thinking is true?

What Socratic questioning is not:

- Getting the client to agree with you ("lip service"). Here is an example of lip service: "Don't you agree with the fact that . . . ?" This is a yes/no question. It does not invite thinking and exploration.
- Manipulating the client to agree with you.
- Getting the client to think exactly like you.

What Socratic questioning is:
Socratic questioning is a process of asking open-ended questions that point your client in the direction of alternative and more realistic ways of thinking about a problem. Socratic questions point in the direction of evidence. It is up to your client to discover the answers to your Socratic questions and the impact that the newly discovered evidence can have on thinking, feelings, and being.
Can't I just tell my client what is wrong with the way he is thinking?
There is no real evidence that telling a client what to think and feel is effective. Just think about yourself: Most of us want a say. We feel that we are right, and if we are not, it may take us some time to make adjustments to the way we think about something. We consider the evidence, sometimes reluctantly, and we adjust our thinking because we are in conversation with someone who cares about us. Our clients are no different. They make changes to their ways of thinking and doing things because they discover new meanings and interpretations in conversation with someone who cares about them.

The Golden Rule of CBT

Listen compassionately. Then ask questions that point your client in the direction of evidence that can change the way he thinks, feels, and behaves.

Building a Treatment Plan for Sheney

Sheney's treatment plan will need to address the following problems as identified in her Diagnostic Evaluation and case conceptualization:

- Cognitive: Decreasing anxious focus, cognitive errors, increasing realistic thoughts about self, others, and the world
- Behavioral: Increased self-care, behavioral activation, decreasing anxious checking behaviors, increasing joyful interactions with children
- Emotional: Increase ability to tolerate anxiety, increase feelings of self-efficacy/confidence

Once again, working collaboratively is paramount. If identification of goals is a problem, go back to the miracle question: What would your life look like if you woke up tomorrow and all of your problems were suddenly gone?

Sheney's treatment plan for the time being may look like this:

Goal 1:

Sheney will decrease anxious thoughts, feelings, and behaviors by taking active steps to manage her life.

Method 1: Sheney will increase self-care and daily living skills.

How are you going to know that Sheney is following her plan/getting better?

This should be concrete. Sheney will need to see a doctor to rule out medical illness. She will need to learn to establish a better sleep schedule. She will also need to learn to take care of her mail and take steps to obtain employment.

Goal 2:

Sheney will increase joyful positive social interactions to decrease anxious thoughts and feelings.

Method 1: Sheney will engage in joyful interactions with her children daily.

Method 2: Sheney will build a supportive group of friends and family and connect with them daily.

You may want to develop a menu of activities that Sheney is willing to engage in, then monitor if she is actually engaging in those activities.

Goal 3:

Sheney will be able to examine and manage anxious thoughts and feelings.

Method 1: Sheney will be able to identify anxious automatic thoughts.

Method 2: Sheney will be able to examine anxious automatic thoughts.

Method 3: Sheney will be able to replace anxious automatic thoughts with more realistic thoughts.

Note that everything in Sheney's treatment plan serves the purpose of helping her decrease her symptoms of anxiety.

Note that you can begin treatment with just Goal 1. A treatment plan is a work in progress and should be adjusted as necessary. Ongoing collaboration is the key to successful treatment planning and treatment. Work on the treatment plan with the client. Say things like:

This is your plan.

Is there anything on your plan that we should change?

What is working for you? What is not working?

What Is the Role of the Therapeutic Relationship in Cognitive Behavioral Therapy?

Beck (1979, p. 27), clearly states that attention must be paid to the therapeutic relationship. CBT is more than a set of techniques. Dobson & Dobson (2017) compare the therapeutic relationship to the "vehicle" (p. 67) that drives change. Tolin (2016, p. 11) references Carl Rogers in calling for empathy, genuineness, and unconditional positive regard.

However, Tolin (2016) also makes it clear "that the therapeutic relationship is *necessary*, but not *sufficient*" (p. 138).

CBT is focused on what is happening in the here and now. In order to help your client, you have to attend to what is happening here and now. You have to attend to the relationship because the relationship drives the change process. In other words: If something is wrong in the relationship between the therapist and the client (i.e., let's say that the relationship is not collaborative and the client does not trust the therapist), then change is unlikely to take place.

Here is a visual representation of the role of the therapeutic relationship in CBT:

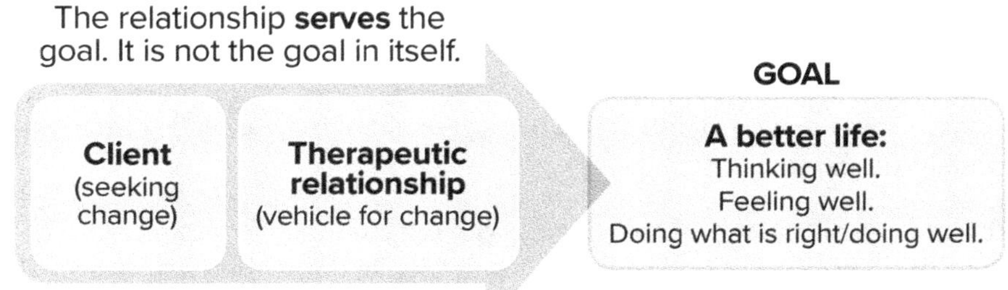

Figure 7

Being Attuned: Building Affect Regulation in the Therapeutic Relationship

Being attuned to your client's emotional state is just as important in CBT as it is in any other form of therapy. Attunement builds the therapeutic relationship.

If your client feels and knows that you are attuned, then she is much more likely to trust you. But just attunement is not enough in CBT.

Let's take a look at the cognitive triad again and how attunement plays a role:

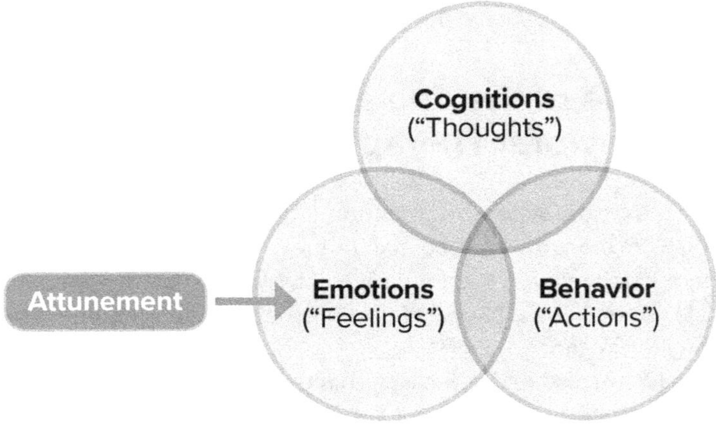

Figure 8

Attunement puts you in touch with your client's emotional state. It gives you an idea of how your client feels. You can then better assess what drives behavior.

You can adjust:

- how you are with your client. You can lower your voice if your client seems agitated and feels threatened but is still unaware of this. You can move your body further away to reduce client feelings of panic/fear.

- what you do with your client: You can offer a blanket or turn on soft music to increase client feelings of safety.

- what you say to your client: You can ask your client if she is feeling threatened/lonely/desperate.

When you are attuning you are working with the emotional component of the cognitive triad. In CBT it is important to always keep in mind how what you are doing (in this case, attuning) fits into the cognitive triad.

Attunement by itself does not "fix" anything. It does help your client feel more comfortable. If your client feels more comfortable and trusts that you are attuned with him and can handle the complex and intense emotions he is feeling, then he is much more likely to be able to move into action.

In other words: If you are attuned with your client, she may be more willing and able to move into work within the cognitive and behavioral component of the cognitive triad. Attunement is an important part of the therapeutic relationship.

What About Co-Regulation?

Co-regulation is a term coined by Allan Schore (2008), the founder of Modern Attachment Theory. Co-regulation is not a CBT term or technique, but understanding it can be helpful when using CBT. Here is a brief definition of co-regulation:

Co-regulation happens when you, the provider, attune with your client. This attunement is initially a right-brain to right-brain process, meaning that it happens naturally. Once you are attuned with your client, once you sense that your client is emotionally dysregulated and may need help with affect regulation, you can help your client regulate.

How does co-regulation happen? Co-regulation is not a verbal process, but it involves a decision on your part, namely to help your client regulate. You may want to breathe slower, relax your body, shift your gaze, or change the tone of your voice. Your state of mind (and body) can have an impact of your client's state of mind and body. You can help your client down-regulate an intense affective state using co-regulation.

When do I use co-regulation? Co-regulatory processes happen in therapeutic and other relationships all the time. You may want to use co-regulation when your client is not ready or able to consciously use words to work to regulate intense affective states (perhaps because no one has modeled this effectively for him).

How does co-regulation fit into the cognitive triad of CBT?

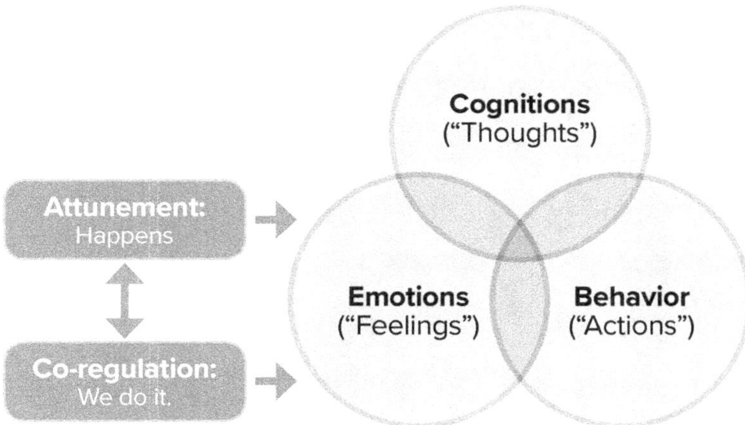

Figure 9

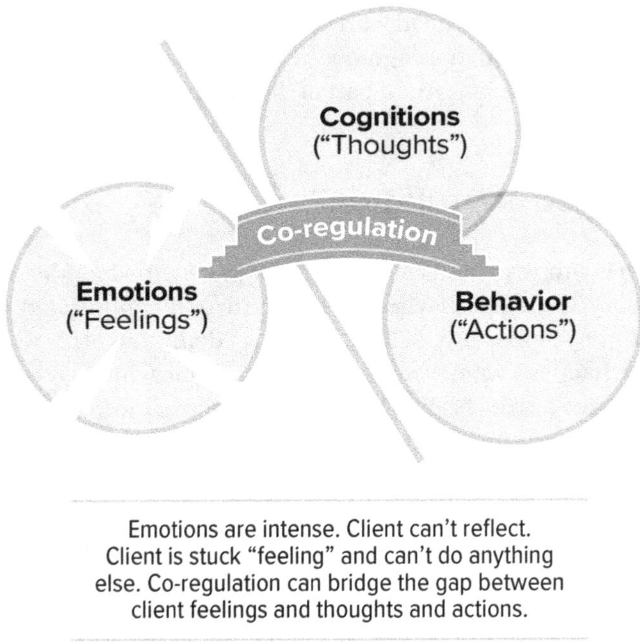

Emotions are intense. Client can't reflect. Client is stuck "feeling" and can't do anything else. Co-regulation can bridge the gap between client feelings and thoughts and actions.

Figure 10

Co-regulation builds the bridge from the emotional component to the cognitive and behavioral component of the cognitive triad. Here is another way of looking at it: When your client is stuck in an emotional state, unable to reflect on it in any way, co-regulation helps her build a connection by moving the emotional part of the cognitive triad back into the triad. You can now do CBT instead of being stuck on work related to feelings only. You could also say that co-regulation gets your client ready to do CBT.

Once your client is back into a more regulated and balanced affective state, she can think, she can act, and she can reflect. Ultimately the experience of co-regulation is meant to implicitly teach self-regulation. If your client already self regulates well, co-regulation is not really needed. Attunement, however, will and should continue to happen.

Client can now connect and reflect.

Figure 11

Just like attunement, co-regulation is used in the service of accessing the full cognitive triad with your client. When you are doing CBT, co-regulation is not enough. It is a means, a vehicle for change.

A word on co-regulation of anxious states of mind:

Before you can help a client regulate an anxious state, you yourself have to be able to regulate your own anxiety. If you are anxious about your client's anxiety, it will be difficult to help her regulate. You have to be able to feel with and for her. Feeling someone else's intense anxiety can be distressing. The key is to feel with the client, to be with the client, but not to make his state of mind and feelings your own.

You are not taking on the client's anxiety, but you are getting to know it so that you can then help her regulate. Interestingly, if you are attuned with your client and you are helping her by co-regulating, she is no longer alone. This in itself can help lift the intense feelings of anxiety.

CBT Techniques and Structure

Sometimes CBT can seem a bit formulaic to a therapist. This can happen when you think of CBT as a set of rules and techniques. You may think that you have to use an automatic thought record if you are doing CBT with a client. Or you may rigidly stick to an established structure for a session when what is needed is some flexibility and attunement.

Tolin (2016, p. 9) uses the analogy of being a chef verses being a cook.

When you are doing CBT: Be a chef. Add your own flavor. Serve what the client is likely going to eat. But also serve something that stretches the client's palate. This is how your client grows.

Keep in mind that you can use many kinds of techniques when doing CBT—as long as this is done within the context of CBT (i.e., as long as you are working with your client on changing cognitions, emotions, and behavior to better fit the reality your client is facing).

Still, there are ways in which CBT is different from other forms of therapy.

CBT is more directive and more structured than other forms of treatment for depression (such as interpersonal psychotherapy). Treatment has a structure. There are things to be learned. Every session has a structure. You can step away from the structure of the session. You can be flexible. But when you are doing so, you are very much aware that you are doing this and why you are doing this. To stick with the culinary analogy: There is a menu. The menu can vary, but there is always a menu. For the treatment of anxiety this makes sense: Anxiety can make your client seemingly aimless. She may have no structure in her days and may anxiously hop from one thought, feeling, and behavior to another. This process can then perpetuate a general anxious state.

CBT creates a structure and a plan for your client. The message to your client is: There is a way out of your anxiety. I can teach you the steps you need to take.

Creating Structure

Treatment has a structure: As Tolin (2016) puts it: "CBT tends to not be a forever, Woody Allen-style treatment" (p. 8).

Why is this so?

Because treatment is focused on the collaboratively established goals, not on other things that come up in the course of treatment/the course of a session. This does not mean that treatment goals can't be revised if this is needed. If a client develops suicidal ideation while in treatment, clearly the treatment plan needs to be revisited and revised.

Is there a prescribed length of treatment?

As client problems vary, so does length of treatment. Dobson & Dobson (2017) reference a 12–16 session length. Clients in the community mental health setting have often experienced a lifetime of toxic stress and multiple traumatic events. Additionally, they may suffer from co-occurring physical and mental illness and substance abuse disorders. When this is the case, treatment will likely require significantly more time. Clients with co-occurring disorders should receive concurrent treatment for their conditions and appropriate services to facilitate recovery and resilience development.

Community Mental Health Practice Alert

Clients in a community mental health setting often present with a multiplicity of symptoms and problems. Our clients are often dually diagnosed. And they are often physically ill. They may have depression and PTSD. They may have lifelong exposure to Toxic Stress.

At OhioGuidestone, more than 55% of our clients may have an ACE Score of 4 or more, putting them at a much higher risk for a variety of physical and mental health problems. What this means is that your client may have anxiety and diabetes or anxiety and heart disease. They may also struggle with an addiction that is diagnosed or undiagnosed.

What does this mean for treatment duration?

If your client struggles with more than one mental health problem and additional physical and environmental problems, it unlikely that treatment duration will fall within the 12–16 week range.

It is important, however, to keep in mind and to discuss with your client that treatment has a course: There is a beginning and an end. The goal of treatment is to resolve the mental health issues that brought your client into treatment. Both you and your client should be aware where you are in the client's treatment. Are you just beginning? Are you in the midst of it? Or are you almost done? You and your client should frequently discuss this.

Once again, creating structure is important. If your client feels that he has so many problems he may never be done with treatment, this could contribute to a sense of anxiety. When using CBT, length of treatment can vary depending on the complexity of symptoms and problems. Structure, however, is a constant.

Creating Structure When Discussing Course and Length of Treatment

You can use a simple visual aid like this to discuss the course and possible length of treatment with your client.

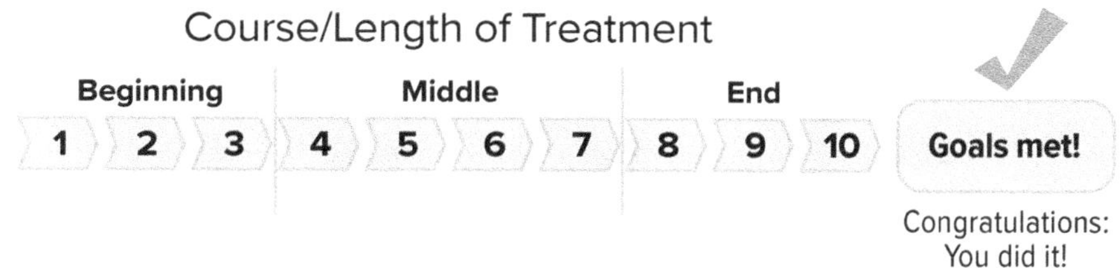

Figure 12

Creating Structure for Each Session

Here is an example of how you can structure a session with your client:

CBT Session Structure

4. Check-In: This is brief, perhaps five minutes. Is there anything new that is relevant to treatment? Has anxiety gotten better, worse, or remained the same?

5. Identify Today's Tasks: Again, this is brief. Identify what needs to be done today. Be collaborative about this. If your client is unfocused and wants to add things that are not relevant to treatment, it is OK to be directive and refer to treatment goals. If new things have come up, help the client evaluate how they fit into treatment and rate how important it is to address them right now. Will they detour treatment, or are they right on track to move the client forward?

6. Homework Review: Homework is an integral component of CBT. Homework brings the content of therapy into the real world. This is where skills will need to be practiced and new ways of thinking/doing/feeling can be tried. Celebrate successes, even the small ones, and problem-solve about things that did not work.

7. Work on Today's Tasks: This is where the "meat" of your session takes place. Be sure to anchor your work in the treatment plan and the cognitive triad. This is where behavioral, emotional, or cognitive work takes place.

8. Summarize the Work: You are the "guide" through treatment and through each session. Summarize periodically what you are talking about and how this fits into treatment progress.

9. Identify New Homework: New homework can originate from the homework review at the beginning of the session and/or today's tasks. You and the client can identify what needs practice. Be sure that homework can realistically be accomplished.

10. Closing: Summarize session takeaways. Clarification of questions. Feedback about session.

Adapted from Persons, Davidson and Tompkins (2001), Essential Components of Cognitive Behavioral Therapy for Depression, APA: Washington, DC.

Here is a simplified version to keep handy for your client as you travel through each session:

CBT Session Structure
Check-In
Identify Today's Task
Homework Review
Work on Today's Task
Summarize the Work
Identify New Homework
Closing

Essential CBT Techniques

Remember, CBT can borrow techniques from a variety of evidence-based forms of therapy such as dialectical behavior therapy (DBT) or acceptance and commitment therapy (ACT). There are, however, a few essential intervention components you should use.

Psychoeducation

Dobson and Dobson (2017) define psychoeducation "as the provision of information about relevant psychological principles and knowledge . . ." (p. 96).

Psychoeducation takes place throughout the course of treatment. At the beginning of treatment, you should provide your client with appropriate information about:

- Anxiety: Symptoms and Treatment

- CBT 101: Go over the cognitive triad (but don't call it that). It is important that your client understands that he will be working on thoughts, feelings, and behaviors and that these are connected. You can also determine together where the client is most willing and able to start work. For many of our clients, behavioral work is the most accessible.

- Explain that CBT is collaborative, structured, focused, and present-oriented.

- Resources: Periodically assess what your client needs. Does he need access to an advocacy or support group? Legal assistance? Job training? Resource building is an important aspect of CBT because increased access to resources gives your client an opportunity to act. As anxiety can lead to frantic and ineffective action or inaction, helping your client build a roadmap for action can be life changing.

Socratic Questioning

Socratic questioning is a process of asking open-ended questions that point your client in the direction of alternative and more realistic ways of thinking about a problem. Socratic questions point in the direction of evidence. It is up to your client to discover the answers to your Socratic questions and the impact that the newly discovered evidence can have on thinking, feelings, and being. Telling your client the answers to the questions you are asking is not effective. In CBT you should be asking a lot of Socratic questions. As tempting as it may be to give your client answers, they would be your answers, not hers.

Homework

Tolin (2016, p. 154) identifies the following kinds of homework:

Reading assignments tailored to the client's specific needs and abilities.

This can be tricky for our clients. Keep in mind that many of our adult clients read on a third- to fifth-grade level. Assess your client's ability to take in written information. Keep it simple. Use handouts that contain visual representations of the information you want your client to review. Reading assignments are, of course, a form of psychoeducation. They are also designed to empower and change the way your client thinks about herself, others, and the world.

Self-Monitoring

You can create simple checklists to help your client monitor problematic behaviors and thoughts. Be sure to explain that self-monitoring is designed to establish a baseline and determine treatment needs. Here is what a simple monitoring chart could look like:

	Mon	Tue	Wed	Thu	Fri	Sat	Sun
Hours in bed							
Hours of TV							

Figure 13

You can use this chart over the course of several weeks to monitor decreased time spent in bed (if this is a goal). Honesty, of course, is key to self-monitoring. Be sure that you collaborate with your client on a realistic goal and a charting system that feels right for her.

Learning and Practicing New Behaviors

Skills Training

New skills will have to be learned together in session, then practiced in the real world. In other words: It is easier to talk about a new skill/new behavior than to engage in it. You should explain to your client that there is no such thing as failure when practicing a new skill or behavior. Each "mistake" will guide both of you to make changes and refine the work. Each "mistake" will help you examine negative automatic thoughts. In other words: Each perceived mistake is a new learning opportunity and guides the way you create change together.

Behavior Changes

Your anxious client may need specific behavior changes. You may want to assign a specific behavior that you want your client to increase. It is a good idea to use a self-monitoring chart to track the new behavior. Be sure to keep it simple and set realistic goals. Instead of asking your client to visit a family member/friend every day, ask your client to contact a family member/friend on three out of seven days. Then identify specifically who your client will contact and make sure that she actually has a valid phone number or address for that person. Here is a simple chart to monitor behavior change:

	Mon	Tue	Wed	Thu	Fri	Sat	Sun
Contacted friend/family member X							

Figure 14

By setting a realistic goal, you are making sure your client can be successful now. This is especially important when she is anxious. Celebrate the small successes with your client, then raise the bar. One way of doing so is to move from the task of contacting a person to the task of spending time with that person (which requires face-to-face contact).

If your client is anxious and you set the bar too high, you run the risk of increasing her anxiety and perhaps even the risk of her not returning to treatment. If you set the bar too low, your client is not learning anything she does not already know or do. The key is to collaborate with your client on defining just the right amount of behavior change: change that challenges her but does not flood her with so much anxiety that she cannot function.

What if my client has no family/friends? Continue to keep in mind how important collaboration is. Know your client! If your client is really and truly completely isolated and has no one in the world to support him, this is an important clinical issue by itself. Go back to resource building. Brainstorm with your client. Find a support/advocacy group. Connect your client with peer supports. All of this creates a path to action.

Behavioral Activation

Because anxiety can create complete inaction (a "freeze" kind of response) or frantic but ineffective action (similar to a "fight" response), your client will have to learn to take a new and different kind of action: realistic and planful action. If she does not learn this, a vicious cycle of anxiety continues:

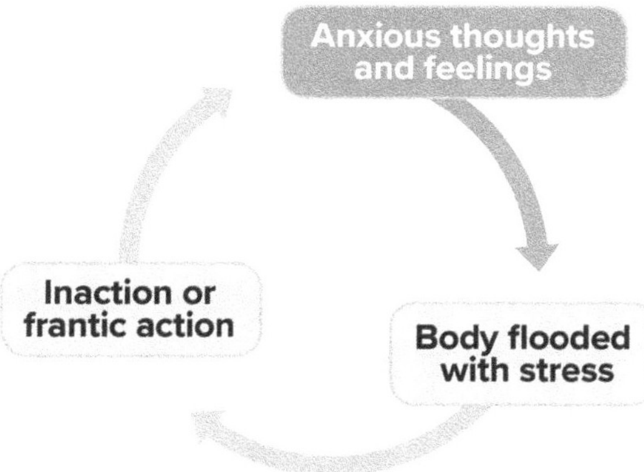

Figure 15

Provide psychoeducation to your client about this cycle. Explain that just by changing one part of the cycle, the whole cycle can begin to change. Express understanding that changing anxious thoughts and feelings can be hard and suggest that you start by changing behaviors, such as scheduling activities and altering the environment (i.e., going new places and seeing new people). Explain that it is OK if activities are not "fun" at first. Explain that over time and with practice enjoyment will return.

Here is what the cycle of behavioral change looks like:

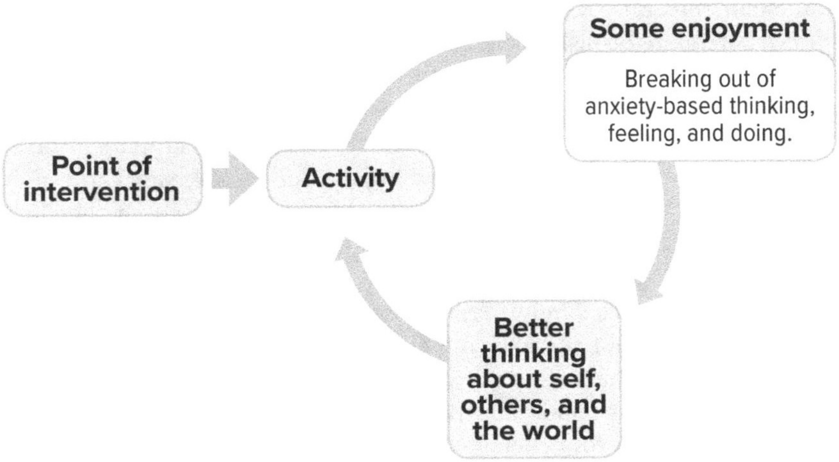

Figure 16

Tolin (2016, p. 224-226) outlines the benefits of activity scheduling and explains that it goes hand-in-hand with self-monitoring. While it is good to be ambitious about behavioral changes and activity scheduling, it is equally important to be realistic about it. You are teaching your client to create achievable and realistic behavioral goals.

Here is a simple Activity Schedule you can use with clients. The further you are in treatment, the more meaningful activities you may want to include.

	Mon	Tue	Wed	Thu	Fri	Sat	Sun
Morning							
Afternoon							
Evening							

Figure 17

Cognitive Restructuring

Let's take another look at the role of thoughts/cognitions in CBT.

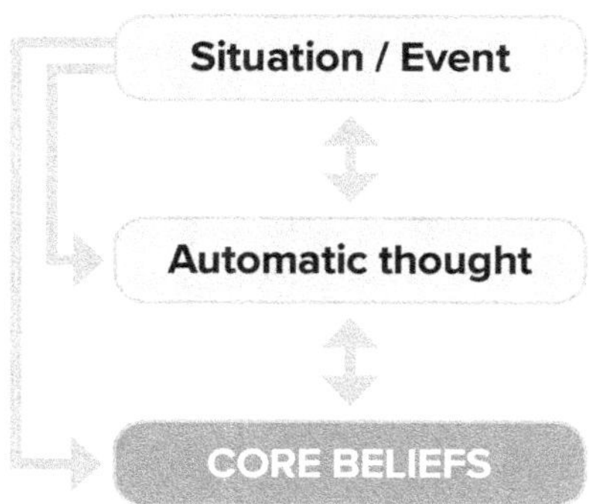

Figure 18: Note that core beliefs are much harder to identify than automatic thoughts. Automatic thoughts just appear; we do not have to ask for them. Because they appear so often, they are easier to bring into conscious awareness.

Negative and faulty core beliefs are at the root of anxious thoughts and feelings. But those core beliefs can be difficult to uncover. They are triggered by a situation or event. Once a core belief is triggered, it sends out its "messengers"—those pesky negative automatic thoughts.

Negative automatic thoughts are much easier to address because they show up all the time and may even "bug" your client.

Here are some examples of automatic thoughts:

- I always mess everything up.

- She hates me.

- I am going to fail this one.

Automatic thoughts can be examined. In CBT you and your client are looking for evidence for and against the truth of the automatic thought.

Here is what this would look like:

A situation or event triggers a negative automatic thought, which in turn will affect negatively the way your client feels. But what if the thought was nothing more than the brain letting off some steam?

If this could happen, then we should be able to examine thoughts and ask: Is this a realistic thought? Or is this just my brain blowing off some steam (you could use the term *brain fart*)?

Automatic Thought	Evidence for AT	Evidence against AT
I mess everything up.	I lost my phone.	• I went to work today. • I found my phone. • My sister called me to ask for advice. • . . .
She hates me.	She is mad at me about the thing I said.	• We have been dating for 6 months. • We make each other laugh. • She called me to talk. • . . .
I am failing.	I failed a spelling test.	• Just got into district art show. • Passing grades, even in spelling. • . . .

Figure 19 (A blank version can be found in the appendix.)

Notice that each of the automatic thoughts outlined above has the potential to make your client more anxious. They can drive your client into frantic action (anxiety), fearful inaction (anxiety/freeze response), or hopeless inaction (depression).

Keep in mind that automatic thoughts can be relentless. Once you have examined them with your client, it is OK to use humor when one shows up. You can talk to an automatic thought! Here is an example:

> *Hello there. There you are again, trying to trick me. Not going to happen. You, my uninvited friend, are just a brain fart. Stinky and unpleasant. I am going to leave you now and think better thoughts. Goodbye!*

Talking to the automatic thought in this way creates distance to it. It is far easier to examine a faulty thought from a distance!

Why do you want your client to examine automatic thoughts?

Because they create feelings based on these faulty automatic thoughts. If your client can dismiss those faulty automatic thoughts, then he can begin to let go of the feelings based on those thoughts.

If you and your client run into a set of automatic thoughts with a similar theme, you are probably on to a core belief. Core beliefs, too, can be examined for their truthfulness.

Cognitive Behavioral Interventions for Anxiety

CBT is a treatment of choice for anxiety disorders. There are some differences within the category of anxiety disorders addressed in this manual. Generalized anxiety disorder, panic disorder, and social phobia can be addressed using a standard CBT approach.

Specific phobias call for a specific CBT approach using exposure therapy. Elements of exposure therapy, such as exposure to anxiety-provoking thoughts or behaviors, can also be helpful when treating other forms of anxiety, such as generalized anxiety or panic disorder.

This manual will address how to treat generalized anxiety disorder, panic disorder, and social anxiety using CBT interventions. There will be distinct interventions for the treatment of specific phobias that must involve exposure therapy. Keep in mind, however, that specific phobias can occur concurrently with other anxiety disorders. If, for example, your client suffers from both generalized anxiety disorder and perhaps a phobia of insects, you will need to discern which symptom is most disabling for the client and begin treatment there.

Here is an example of what this may look like:

- Your client shakes at the thought of coming into contact with any insect. Now she does not leave the house because there could be insects "out there." Your client is also anxious about many other aspects of her life, such as her performance at work, her relationships, and her future.

- Your client's phobia of insects is impacting all other aspects of her life. If she can't leave the house, she will not be able to support herself. Treat the specific phobia right away, then move into treatment of her generalized anxiety disorder.

You should always have the following materials handy for use in session:

- a large variety of art materials, including scissors, tape, and glue;

- comfort items such as pillows, stuffed animals, fidgets; and

- paper and index cards.

If you need more specific materials, they will be listed at the beginning of the intervention.

Cognitive Interventions for Anxiety Disorders

Changing behaviors based on anxious thoughts and feelings can be as difficult as it can be liberating. It may be helpful to begin with changing your client's anxious thoughts. Anxious thoughts inevitably give birth to more anxious thoughts unless your client views hers differently and learns to examine them.

INTERVENTION 1

My Name is Failure

This intervention addressed a fundamental anxious thought: The "no matter what I do, I will fail" kind of thought. Ironically, because this thought can provoke more anxious feelings and lead to either frantic but ineffective action or inaction (freeze response), the thought can become a self-fulfilling prophecy. Because I think that I will fail, my actions do not "fit" the situation, and I become much less effective in what I do.

Target skill: Evaluating thoughts. Adaptive thinking.

1. Begin with empathy. Ask about your client's anxious thoughts. Say: *It must be so hard to have these thoughts all the time.*

2. While doing so, begin to frame your client's thoughts as just some among many. Ask about any self-affirming thoughts your client may have. If she struggles with this, dig deep. If she thinks she can't do anything right, how did she get to your office? Clearly, she has some competence.

3. Identify today's task: examining and putting anxious thoughts into place.

4. Work on today's task. Begin with psychoeducation: Explain that the brain produces thoughts at a rapid rate and that some are more important than others. Here are some examples you could name:

Nonsense Thought	Anxious Thought	(Overly) Optimistic Thought	Realistic Thought
Flying monkeys are about to invade.	I think that this will not go well.	This will be terrific. Nothing can stand in my way.	It might be hard. I might be afraid, but I can to this.

Figure 21

5. Ask your client to identify at least one of her thoughts in each category. If your client is struggling with depression and/or anxiety, realistic and optimistic thoughts will be difficult to name. This is OK.

6. If you are working with a child or a creative adult, your client can illustrate her thoughts.

7. Spend some time exploring with your client how she views her thoughts. Ask Socratic questions about the "truth" of her thoughts. Here are some examples:

  - *How do you respond to an anxious thought?*
  - *What happens when an anxious thought turns into a nonsense thought?*
  - *What happens when your client tries to be very optimistic and things do not work out?*
  - *What does it mean to think realistically?*

8. By asking these questions, you have established that anxious (and other) thoughts can be examined.

9. Move into examining the anxious thought about failure. Ask:

  - *When does your anxious thought about failure turn into a nonsense thought?*
  - *In what way is your anxious thought unrealistic?*
  - *In what way does your anxious thought relate to reality?*
  - *What is your experience with anxious thoughts? What do they make you do?*

10. Show your client the following image:

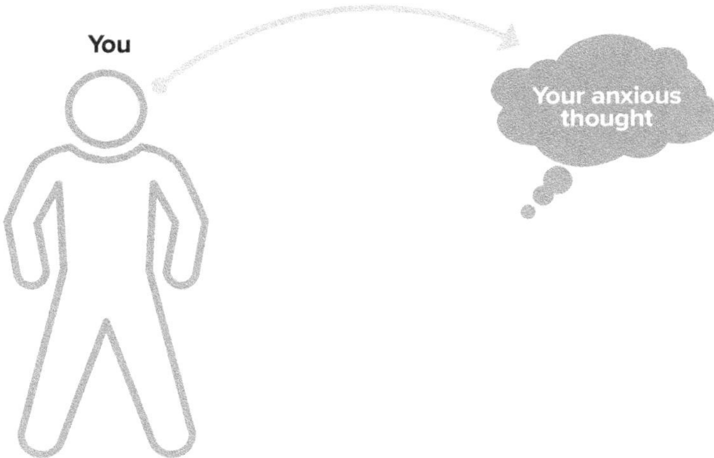

Figure 22

11. Explain: *You can examine your terrible anxious thought of failure. You are in charge. You can sort thoughts into categories such as "nonsense thoughts" and "anxious thoughts."*

12. Say: *You are more than your thoughts. You produce thoughts, you contain thoughts, but you are also so much more than your thoughts.*

13. Go back to the thought: "I am a failure." Ask your client to put that in its place using the following image:

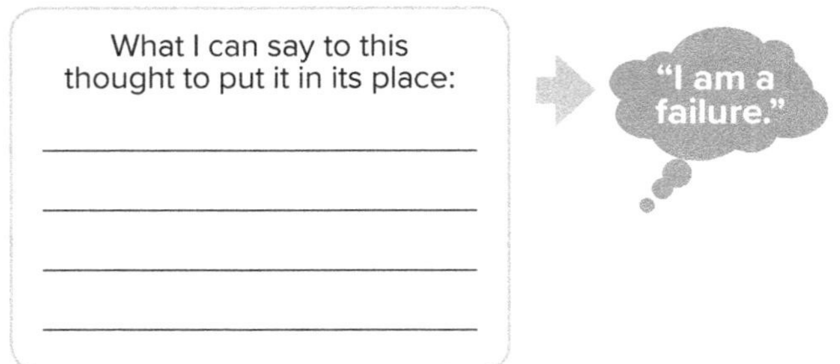

Figure 23

14. Summarize what you have done so far. You have learned that the brain produces all kinds of thoughts, not all of which are of equal value and importance. You have identified examples for all kinds of thoughts. You have established that your client is in charge of her thoughts and can put them into place, and you have "talked back" to the thought "I am a failure."

15. Identify homework: Ask your client to take home an index card with the image she created above. Ask your client to use the index card when she has thoughts of failure, and "talk back" to those thoughts using the examples she has already identified. She should bring the card back to your next meeting.

16. Closing: Explain that you have learned to look at thoughts from afar and that by doing this, your client can make them feel less overwhelming. Make sure your client understands the homework.

17. What if your client "talks back" to the anxious thought but is just going through the motions and does not believe what she says? Give it time. This way of thinking about thoughts may be new for her. She may be attached to the "truth" of her thoughts. Right now, you are just trying to establish that it is possible to think differently.

INTERVENTION 2

Rotten Tomato Thoughts

This intervention builds on what your client has already learned. Thoughts can be examined and categorized. Your client has learned this and practiced putting thoughts into their place. The following intervention will help your client learn about the concept of automatic thoughts. This will help her understand that it is the nature of certain thoughts to show up over and over again. She will then be able to plan ahead for responding to repetitive thought in a helpful manner.

Target skill: Understanding and evaluating automatic thoughts.

1. Begin with empathy. Ask your client about her week. What went well? What did not? Listen for anxious thoughts and, when they come up, help your client label them as such. Do so in a careful manner. You don't want your client to think that you are dismissing her thoughts. You are not. You are just putting them in their place and calling them what they are.

2. Identify today's task: figuring out what to do with pesky, rapid-fire, and repetitive anxious thoughts. Ask your client about her repetitive thoughts: What does it feel like when they come? How does she respond to them (both behaviorally and emotionally)?

3. Homework review: Look at last week's index card with your client. Ask her if and when she used it. Was she able to talk back to pesky thoughts? And if she was, what did that feel like? Did she feel empowered? Or perhaps guilty? Did she struggle with believing herself when talking back? Explain that all of these responses are normal and that it can be difficult to change deeply ingrained ways of thinking, but this does not mean that they can't be changed.

4. Work on today's task: Begin with psychoeducation to help your client understand the nature of pesky anxious thoughts. You can use the following image:

Figure 24

Stupid . . . lazy . . . never gonna work . . . why are you even . . . this will never work . . .

You get the idea. Explain that this kind of thinking can wear you down and make itself seem logical after a while.

5. Explain that anxiety, just like depression, can be a liar and a con man. It can trick you into thinking and believing something by repeating a lie over and over.

6. Explain that anxious automatic thoughts of failure can be examined using evidence. You can use the following chart to help your client examine the evidence for and against her automatic thoughts:

Automatic Thought	Evidence for AT	Evidence against AT
I mess everything up. Rotten Tomato Thought	I lost my phone.	• I went to work today. • I found my phone. • My sister called me to ask for advice. • . . .
She hates me.	She is mad at me about the thing I said.	• We have been dating for 6 months. • We make each other laugh. • She called me to talk. • . . .
I am failing.	Failed spelling test.	• Just got into district art show. • Passing grades, even in spelling. • . . .

Figure 25

Be creative and let your client complete the chart any way she can, drawing or writing. If your client struggles with writing, you can be her scribe. Support your client in identifying evidence against her automatic thought of failure.

7. If it helps your client, ask her to think of automatic thoughts of failure as spoiled food. You can say: *Would you really want to eat this rotten tomato? Not only is it rotten, it's quite smelly, too.*

8. Provide your client with an image of a rotten tomato.

    Ask: *Would you eat this? If not, then why listen to a rotten thought? If someone offered you ten rotten tomatoes, would you eat them just because there are many of them?*

    Then ask: *Where do rotten tomatoes belong?* Take the metaphor as far as your client can. Perhaps she wants to throw them in the garbage. Or perhaps she wants to take them out to the compost where they can turn into something useful.

Figure 26

9.	Summarize what you have done so far:

- You have examined the nature of anxious automatic thoughts.
- You have determined that just because there are many and they come in rapid succession does not mean that they contain truth.
- You have labeled those kind of thoughts "rotten tomato thoughts."
- You have determined that you would not eat one rotten tomato, let alone a whole bunch of them. You have thought about what to do with rotten tomatoes and rotten tomato kind of thoughts: They can go in the garbage or be composted.

10.	Identify new homework. Ask your client to carry a rotten tomato index card with her. If your client is a child or a creative adult, she may want to draw her own rotten tomato and glue it on an index card. Ask your client to look at the card every time an anxious automatic rotten tomato kind of thought comes along and say out loud: *That's a rotten tomato thought. I'm not buying it, and I'm not eating it.*

11.	Closing: Review with your client that the purpose of calling her anxious thoughts of failure rotten tomato thoughts is to help her distance herself from thoughts that are not worth much. Reassure her that she has plenty of valuable and realistic thoughts. If your client has questions, answer them.

INTERVENTION 3

Finding a Place for Anxious Thoughts

This intervention will identify another way of putting anxious thoughts in their place. It does not deny their existence but encourages exiling them. CBT does not ask your client to not have anxious thoughts. That would be impossible. CBT asks your client to examine thoughts to determine how realistic they are and then manage them based on that judgment.

Target skill: Evaluating and containing automatic thoughts.

1. Begin with empathy. Check in with your client about her level of anxiety. How anxious has she been over the past few days? What has she been able to do in spite of her anxiety?

2. Identify today's task: finding a place for those anxious automatic thoughts that just keep on coming. Ask: *What would it be like to change your thinking about these thoughts? What if it would be possible to find a place to put those thoughts, to contain them?*

3. Review homework: Ask your client if she has used her Rotten Tomato Index Card over the past few days. Has she taken it out when she has had an anxious, unrealistic thought? What was it like to call that thought a rotten tomato thought? Did it feel liberating? Silly? How did talking back to her anxious thought change her relationship with it?

4. Work on today's task: Begin by asking your client to name a specific anxious and unrealistic thought that is bugging her today. It should be one that comes up frequently and impacts how she feels and acts. Here is an example of that kind of thought:

   I am about to be fired because I looked at my boss the wrong way. I am such a loser. I might as well stay home today because I am going to get fired anyway.

5. Give your client a rough drawing of a house and herself. Here is an example you can use. If you are working with a child or a creative adult, they may want to create the drawing themselves.

Figure 27

6. Now: Ask your client to envision taking that anxious pesky thought and walking it over to the house. Ask her to open the door and release the anxious thought into the house. You can use a script like this:

> *Take that thought, that thought that is making you anxious, the thought that you are going to get fired. Think of it as a little thought cloud. Hold it in your hand and walk it over to the house. Open the door and place the thought in the house. Then close the door.*
>
> *Walk away. You can turn around. The thought is still there, but it is contained in the house. You might be looking at it but through the glass. It is behind a window. It is a thought. It has a place to live, but you just won't let it take up space in your brain.*

7. What if another anxious thought shows up? Walk that one over, too. If your client has a lot of anxious automatic thoughts, you may want to add another house to the picture. If your client is creative, let her do this.

8. What if my client has objections? She may say something like: **My thoughts can't really live in a house.** This is true, of course. Explain to your client that you are simply trying to find a way to think differently about anxious thoughts. Thoughts are not things. They are real but not tangible. Thought are realistic or not. Ask your client to find some other way to contain thoughts. She may come up with a different drawing. This is OK as long as she puts those thoughts in their place.

9. Look at the image you have created together: What does it feel like to contain thoughts symbolically? Is it OK for your client to try to find a way to contain her thoughts?

10. Summarize the work: You have identified an anxious and bothersome thought. You have walked that thought over to its own place and put it in there to contain it. It does not mean that it is gone; it is just contained. It no longer takes up brain and emotional space. You have discussed how, if necessary, this process can be repeated. New houses can be drawn if needed. You have explored what it feels like to contain anxious thoughts and walk away from them without denying their existence.

11. Identify new homework: Send home the drawing you have created together. Ask your client to post it in a prominent place, if possible, such as over the kitchen table or next to the bathroom mirror. Ask your client to add to the drawing over the next few days. She can use thought clouds to put more thoughts into the house. Here are a few:

Figure 28

She may also want to draw different paths to the house(s). Sometimes it may be difficult to contain an anxious thought, and she may take a detour to get to the house. Some thoughts may require a tower to contain them. Ask your client to be creative and reinforce that thinking about thoughts and ways to contain them can be fun. Ask your client to bring the drawing to your next meeting.

12. Closing: Make sure that your client understands the idea of symbolically containing anxious thoughts. Ask her if she has any questions and send her home with the assignment of containing her anxious thoughts.

INTERVENTION 4

Visiting Anxious Thoughts

This intervention builds on the previous one, meaning your client should be familiar with the idea of symbolic containment of anxious thoughts. Your client will learn that once anxious thoughts are contained, they can be visited. Your client does not have to be anxious about anxious thoughts (anticipatory anxiety), but rather can choose to interact with them.

Target skill: Facing and coping with anxious thoughts.

1. Begin with empathy. Ask your client about her anxious thoughts over the past few days. How intrusive were they? What was your client able to do in spite of them?

2. Identify today's task for your client: learning to "visit" anxious thoughts without fear. Bring up the idea that anxious thoughts can be symbolically contained. Explain that, once thoughts are contained, they can seem less frightening and may be easier to visit.

3. Review the homework: Look at the image your client brought back to you. Ask her if she hung the picture in her home. What has she added to the image and why? Did anyone comment on the image and, if they did, what did they say? How does she feel about the idea of containing anxious thoughts? Has this had an impact on how she manages them? If your client wants to add to the image or make changes as you are talking, this is OK.

4. Work on today's task: Keep the image of your client's anxious thoughts contained in a house out in the open. Now, ask your client what it would be like to visit one of those anxious thoughts and talk to it. What would she say to the anxious thought? Would she be scared to talk to it if she knew she could put it back in the house and leave? What if the anxious thought talks back or tries to pull her into the house?

5. Work with your client on developing a list of things she would like to say to her anxious thoughts. Here are some examples:

Things I want to ask my anxious thoughts/tell my anxious thoughts:
You don't rule me.
What are you trying to tell me?
Why should I listen to you?

Figure 29

6. Be sure to help your client to include things that put the anxious thought into place. Explain that it is not necessary to "be mean" to the anxious thought, but it is necessary to be truthful to it. It's OK to tell the anxious thought that it is a liar!

7. Now: Ask your client to role play the conversation with the anxious thought, using the list of things that your client has created. At first, your client will be the anxious thought, and you will say the things your client wants to say to it. Feel free to elaborate more when you talk back to the anxious thought. The point is to give your client words to put the anxious thought into its place.

8. Then switch. You will be the anxious thought, and your client will try to put it into its place. It's quite possible that this is still difficult for your client. This is OK. Tell her that she is practicing and that practice makes perfect.

9. Once you are done role playing, help your client reflect on the experience. You can ask the following questions:

   - *Was it easier to be the anxious thought or refute the anxious thought?*
   - *What did it feel like to talk back to the anxious thought?*
   - *What are thoughts to you right now?*
   - *Are you able to examine a thought as a thought?*
   - *In what way do anxious thoughts still frighten you? In what way do they not?*
   - *Do you think it is possible to be kind to an anxious thought?*

10. Stay within the symbolism of today's intervention. When you are done, ask your client to put the anxious thought back in the house, close the door, then walk away. To reinforce this you can say something like:

    Now that you have talked to your anxious thought and have told it all it needs to know, it is time to send it back to its own home. "Farewell, anxious thought. I will now take you and put you back in your house. I am closing the door, and I am walking away. Perhaps I will come back when I want to, but for now I am leaving."

11. Summarize what you have done together today: You have explored the idea and practice of visiting an anxious thought and talking to it on the client's terms. She has learned that it is OK to question an anxious thought, and that not all of them are true. She has also learned to be less afraid of her anxious thought, which ultimately will mean less anticipatory anxiety.

12. Assign new homework: Ask your client to talk back to bothersome anxious thoughts in the following way using an index card you send home with her. She should carry this card with her and take it out and read it when anxious bothersome thoughts keep her from moving forward.

    Hello there, anxious thought. There you are again. I recognize you. I recognize that you are trying to bother me. To get me to give up. To not believe in myself.

Guess what: I hear you, but I don't believe you. Even if you repeat yourself —and I understand that you often do—I still don't believe you.

I am putting you back in your house where you belong. Goodbye!

13. What if your client thinks that she won't believe herself when she talks back to her anxious thought? Tell your client that it is OK. She is practicing. She also can ask a person who is close to her to read the script to her. It is often easier to take in something new and kind from another person at first.

14. Closing: Say things like:

- *Today you have learned to visit your anxious thoughts on your own terms.*

- *You have been able to say what you needed and wanted to say. Good for you. You can practice this at home now. Give it a try.*

If your client has any questions, answer them.

INTERVENTION 5

Inviting In the Anxious Thought

This intervention takes a different approach to relating to anxious, unrealistic thoughts. Perhaps they do not need not need to be exiled because they are just thoughts. Perhaps it is possible to "invite them in" because they have no power other than the power we give them. If you have determined with a client that a thought is not realistic, but it keeps coming up, perhaps we should invite it in—it is going to show up anyway!

Target skill: Welcoming, tolerating, and coping with anxious thoughts.

1. Check in with your client. Ask about her level of anxiety during the past few days. You can use the following image to help your client determine her level of anxiety.

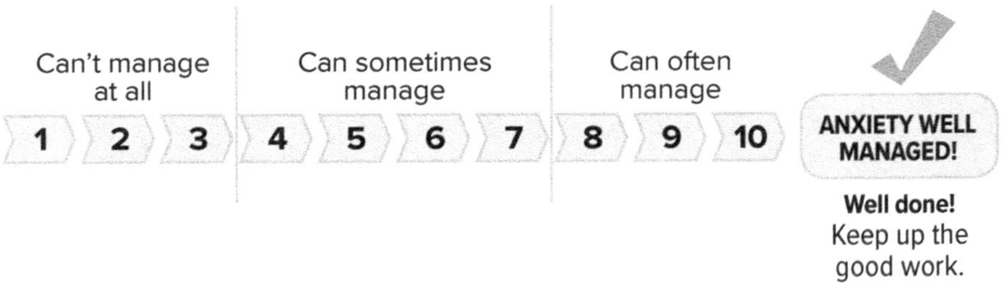

Figure 30

    Explain to your client that today's check-in is not about how well she is doing in her treatment (that would create more anxiety), but rather about helping her to start looking at her levels of anxiety at different times.

2. Identify today's task: inviting anxiety in, as opposed to trying to push it away and keep it at bay. Explain that for some, the idea of containment works well, but that it can also be a good idea not to "fight" anxious thoughts. If they are not realistic, then they hold no power other than the power we give them.

3. Review the homework: Did your client carry her index card with her? Did she remember to take it out when anxious bothersome thoughts came up? Did she use the card and read it out loud to herself? If she did, what did it feel like? Did it make a difference in the way she related to her anxious thought? Or did she ask a friend to read the card to her? If she did, what was it like to enlist the help of a friend? How did she feel after her friend read the card to her? Did it make a difference in the way she related to her anxious thoughts?

4. Work on today's task: inviting anxiety into the room. Letting it in without hesitation and fear. Listening to it without believing its message.

By now you are probably familiar with the specific anxious thoughts your client has. You are going to role play with her. Initially you will be the client and your client will be her anxious thoughts.

5. Here is what this conversation may sound like:

> **You:** Sounds like there is a knock at the door. That's probably my anxious thoughts. Hello there, come on in and have a seat.

> **Anxious Thoughts (as played by your client):** You are as stupid as I thought you are. You are inviting me in? What a fool you are. Well, now I am here just to remind you that there is no way anyone likes you. Really, no way!

> **You:** Interesting thought. I think I understand what you are trying to say. Tell me more!

> **Anxious Thoughts:** Joe does not like you. You know that because he has not called in three days. Eva gave you that look the other day, you know, the "I hate you" look.

> **You:** This is all very interesting. I hear what you are saying, but it doesn't sound right. Joe is not the kind of guy who calls every day, and Eva was having a tough day. These things were not about me.

> **Anxious Thoughts:** Everything is about you. You did this. You said the wrong thing and made them hate you!

You get the idea. Be creative. Don't deny that anxious thoughts are real in that they exist. Listen to them. Give them room, but make it clear that you do not believe them.

6. Now: Switch roles. You, the therapist, will represent the anxious thoughts, and your client's job is to listen to the anxious thoughts without believing them and to tell them what is really going on.

7. When you are done with both versions of role play, help your client reflect on the experience by asking Socratic questions:

- *How difficult was it for her to welcome the anxious thoughts, to let them in?*
- *What was it like to represent the anxious thoughts?*
- *What was it like to talk back to them without fear?*
- *Perhaps this exercise was anxiety provoking?* Ask about this!

8. Summarize what you have done together: You have entertained the idea of inviting in anxious thoughts. You have role-played inviting in anxious thoughts, and your client has experienced both what it is like to represent anxious thoughts and to speak calmly to them.

9. Explain that the purpose of the exercise was to experience a sense of mastery over anxious thoughts—to experience them as "just thoughts."

10. Identify new homework: Ask your client to "sit with" an anxious thought. It is best to identify the anxious thought before she goes home. It should be a medium-level anxious thought, not a terrifying one. Ask your client to set aside two minutes at the end of each day at a specific time to sit with that thought. You should set a time together before your client leaves.

    Explain that sitting with the thought means that she should invite it in, talk to it, and observe it. Once the two minutes are over, she should simply say "goodbye" to the thought and go about her evening. You can give your client this simple chart to keep track of the exercise:

	Thought I am going to sit with:	Daily time:	Done
Mon			
Tue			
Wed			
Thu			
Fri			
Sat			
Sun			

Figure 31

  Ask your client to use the back of the chart to keep track of her emotional responses to sitting with anxious thoughts.

11. If your client is afraid, set a baseline. How long does your client think she can sit with an anxious thought? If she can handle it for fifteen seconds, then that is baseline, and you simply ask her to sit for only fifteen seconds every day.

12. What if your client is still scared to do this? Ask her if a friend can sit with her!

13. Closing: Explain again that today's meeting was about letting anxious thoughts be anxious thoughts without experiencing them as a threat or buying into their message. Check to see if your client has any questions about "inviting in" and "sitting with" anxious thoughts.

INTERVENTION 6

Popping Anxious Bubbles

This intervention encourages your client to think about anxiety as a bubble. It can be shiny, but it has no substance. There is no truth in it. It's just a bubble, and its lure goes away when it's popped.

Target skill: Examining and coping with anxious thoughts. Gauging intensity of anxious thoughts.

1. Check in with your client. Help her gauge her level of anxiety using the simple scaling arrow introduced during the last session.

Figure 32

Ask:

Has anything changed over the last week?

Are you feeling more anxious or less anxious?

If you are feeling more anxious: What thoughts may have triggered this?

If you are feeling less anxious: What did you think or do to decrease your anxiety?

1. Identify today's task: thinking of anxious thoughts as bubbles that can be popped. Explain that because bubbles are shiny, they call attention to themselves, just like anxious thoughts that seem important. Also, the more breath we put into a bubble, the bigger it gets. Similarly, the more attention you pay to an unrealistic worry, the bigger it may seem.

2. Review last week's homework: Look at your client's homework chart together. Did your client take time to sit with a worry? Ask her what this felt like. Did two minutes seem like a long time or a short time? In what way did sitting with the anxious thought change her relationship with it? If your client asked a friend to sit with her, commend her for doing so. Did this make a difference?

3. Work on today's task. You will need a piece of paper with many bubbles on it. Perhaps something like this:

Figure 33

Ask your client to write a worry into each bubble. If your client has the same worry over and over, it can be written into several bubbles.

4. Now: Ask your client what she sees when she looks at the image. In all likelihood she is going to say something like: *All I see is anxious thoughts, so many of them!*

5. Now ask your client to think what may be behind the bubbles. Can she see what is behind them?

6. Help your client reflect on the fact that the bubbles hide what may be behind them. In terms of anxious thoughts, this can mean that we don't see life as it really is because of all the anxious thought bubbles.

7. Use Socratic questions to help your client understand what she may be missing because of her anxious thoughts. Here are some sample questions:

    *   *When you spend your evening worrying, what are you not doing?*

    *   *When you have anxious thoughts about your relationship, who are you not talking to?*

    *   *When you worry about your health, what are you not taking care of?*

8. If you are working with a child or a creative adult, you now get to pop some bubbles. Ask your client to blow a whole bunch of bubbles and think of them as her worries, then ask her to pop these bubbles using a pencil.

9. Some interesting things might happen: Your client may miss a bubble, and it may float away. No problem: Sometimes anxious thoughts do float away. Some bubbles just pop by themselves before we can get to them. Also, no problem. If an anxious thought pops by itself, that's helpful.

10. If your client does not feel like popping bubbles, simply talk about it. There is not much to an anxious thought. It's just a bubble. We make it bigger by paying attention to it and giving it power. But it is really just a bubble.

11. Help your client reflect on what it means to chase the anxious thought bubble. How can she pop the bubble to see the world and live life?

12. Summarize what you have done today: You have explored how anxious thoughts can be like bubbles. They are so shiny that we pay attention to them. But they really do not have much substance and can keep us from seeing reality.

13. Assign new homework: Ask your client to take her bubble drawing home. She should pick one of her anxious thoughts and try to pop it every day. Ask her to be creative. She can:

    - tell the anxious thought that it has no real content;

    - blow the anxious thought away by immersing herself in life;

    - play with the anxious thoughts (bubbles) until they lose their power;

    - watch the anxious thoughts float away; and

    - include a friend and actually pop bubbles. This could be fun. When she is having fun, she is less likely to be worried.

14. Closing: Ask your client what it was like to play with the idea that anxious thoughts are just like bubbles. Did she like being playful about this? If your client has any questions, address them before she leaves.

INTERVENTION 7

Disproving Anxious Thoughts

This is a classic CBT Intervention using a thought record to help your client find evidence to evaluate how realistic thoughts are. Thought records can be dull, but you can bring them to life. There are many ways of doing this:

- Find a song for every thought.
- Identify a TV show that represents the thought.
- Find or create an image for every thought.

Remember, the more your client connects with the activity, the more she will learn from it.

There are many ways to complete the thought-record booklet. It can be done quickly in one session or over the course of two to four. If you are spreading things out, combine pages two and three. You do not want your client to go home with just the page listing evidence for the anxious automatic thought (see below). This would only reinforce it.

Target skill: Recording and coping with anxious thoughts using a thought record.

1. Check in and begin with empathy. What went well over the last week? What did not go well? Use the scaling arrow to help your client gauge her level of anxiety. Are things moving in the right direction? If they are not, be encouraging and embody hope. Explain that anxiety can be pesky. Say: *It has been with you for a while, and it will take a while to learn to manage it. This is OK.*

2. Identify today's task: disproving anxious thoughts using a thought record. Explain that a thought record asks you to:

    - state your anxious thoughts,
    - state the evidence for your anxious thoughts,
    - state the evidence against your anxious thoughts, and
    - find and adopt a more realistic thought.

3. Review last week's homework: Did your client look at her anxious thought bubble image at home? Was she able to look at one bubble daily and try to pop it by talking to it or involving a friend? Was there some enjoyment in popping those bubbles?

4. Work on today's task: creating a thought record to change anxious thinking. You should first help your client identify a particularly pesky anxious thought, one that wreaks havoc in her life. Here is an example of a thought record:

Automatic Thought	Evidence for AT	Evidence against AT
I mess everything up.	I lost my phone.	• I went to work today. • I found my phone. • My sister called me to ask for advice. • . . .
She hates me.	She is mad at me about the thing I said.	• We have been dating for 6 months. • We make each other laugh. • She called me to talk. • . . .
I am failing.	Failed spelling test.	• Just got into district art show. • Passing grades, even in spelling. • . . .

Figure 34

In order to make this a bit more fun, let's break down the thought record into several pages and create a thought-record booklet. Every page will be illustrated by your client in some way.

- Page 1: The pesky anxious thought.

- Page 2: How I think I know that the pesky anxious thought is true.

- Page 3: How I know that the pesky anxious thought is not true.

(Page 2 and Page 3 must be done together)

- Page 4: Adjusted realistic thought: How things really are.

5. Have your client work on each page and illustrate it using whatever art materials she likes. She can write, draw, or create a collage. She can even pick a character from a movie or book that represents her thoughts. Or she can use song lyrics.

6. While your client is working on creating the thought-record booklet, be sure to ask her Socratic questions about her thoughts. Your client may need help with identifying evidence against the anxious automatic thought. Here are some sample questions:

- *What would your best friend say about this thought?*

- *When you are having a great day, what would you say about this thought or to this thought?*

- *What would change for you if this thought was not realistic?*

7. Engage with your client while she continues to work on her automatic thought booklet. Anxious automatic thoughts may come up in the course of creating it, such as:

    - *This looks awful.*

    - *I am terrible at this.*

    Point out that these are examples of anxious automatic thoughts!

8. Once your client has completed the booklet, help her reflect on every page. Again, use Socratic questions to help her understand how changing the way she thinks and examining anxious thoughts can positively impact her life. You can ask "What if . . ." questions like:

    - *What if this thought was not true or realistic?*

    - *What if this thought has been lying to you?*

    - *What if this thought is not really interested in you, but just in itself?*

9. Summarize what you have done together: You have created a thought-record booklet detailing the anxious thought and evidence for and against it. You have identified a better, more realistic thought and explored how it could change your client's life.

10. Assign new homework: Send the thought-record booklet home with your client. Ask her to continue to work on it and to share it with one person she trusts. She should ask this person what he or she thinks about the anxious thought as well as the better and more realistic thought. Ask your client to write down what her friend said on the back of those pages and bring the booklet back to your next meeting.

    If your client has no friends, ask her to pick her favorite person (even if this person is no longer part of her life) and imagine what he or she would say. Spirituality can be helpful, too. Ask what your client's higher power would say to her.

11. Closing: Make sure to ask if your client has any questions. Emphasize that it is OK to have fun with the thought-record booklet. The more colorful, the better!

INTERVENTION 8

One More Page

This intervention builds on the previous one, the automatic thought-record booklet, and adds another page. You will ask your client to consider what her life would be like if she were to adopt more realistic thinking and let go of anxious thoughts. In essence, you are asking your client to think and dream about the future. This will help her build motivation to move towards realistic thinking.

Target skill: Looking to the future. Dreaming.

1. Check in with your client. Use the scaling arrow to help her gauge her level of anxiety and her ability to examine and manage anxious thoughts. When has she been able to manage her anxious thoughts in the past week? What worked? When was this difficult and why? Reinforce the idea that thoughts are just thoughts and that they can be examined.

2. Identify today's task: adding a page to the thought-record booklet. This page will paint the picture of what life will be like when your client adopts more realistic thinking and is able to let go of faulty anxious thoughts. Explain that it can be important to envision a life that is not based on anxious thoughts and ask:

    > *What will be added to your life when anxious thoughts lose their power?*
    > *And what will no longer be a part of your life?*

3. Review last week's homework: Look at your client's thought-record booklet. What has she added and why? Ask if she shared the booklet with anyone. Was it fun to keep working on it? Or did she avoid working on it? Review with your client that she can examine her thoughts and that some do not correspond with reality because they are not supported by evidence.

4. Work on today's task: Adding a page to the thought-record booklet. Give your client an empty page titled "Now: My Life when I don't believe anxious thoughts." Provide art materials and explain that your client can write, draw, create a collage, or do whatever works for her.

5. This is a good time to explain that you are asking your client to think and dream big and realistically. What does she want to do, and what can she do when no longer driven by anxious thoughts? If you are working with a child you may want to explain it in this manner:

    *   *If you no longer worry about other kids not liking you, what would that be like, and who would be around you?*

    *   *It's not about the stuff you want. It's about the life you want.*

    *   *Where do you picture yourself? Who is with you? What are you doing?*

6. It's OK to give your client some leeway with this. You just don't want the entire page to be about "stuff." You can also say: *This is about who you really are when the thick layer of anxiety that covers you right now is peeled away.*

7. If your client struggles with this, ask her to dream about her life without anxious thoughts and create a record of those dreams. If unrealistic things show up on the page, you can explore this with your client later.

8. Now ask your client to explain what is in the picture. Observe her body language and facial expressions. Give her feedback like:

    - *I am noticing a smile on your face when you talk about having a dog.*

    - *You really looked at me when you talked about visiting your brother.*

9. You can call this page your client's motivation page. Say: *You are on your way to this. These are all things that can really happen.*

10. Summarize what you have done today: Your client has added a page to her thought- record booklet. This page shows her realistic dreams—the things, events, and people she wants in her life. Ask her how she feels about what she has created.

11. Assign new homework: Ask your client to take the page home and post it in a prominent place, such as by the bathroom mirror or the kitchen table. Ask her to look at the image once every day at a designated time for a minute or so and take in the details. If she wants to, she can add to the page or show it to a friend. Tell her to look at the image as a source of inspiration and tell herself that all of the things she envisioned are actually possible. Ask her to bring the page back to her next meeting with you.

12. Closing: Before your client leaves, be sure to answer any questions. Compliment her on creating a realistic vision for her life. Explain that this is an ongoing process and that it is likely her vision will expand and change over time as her anxiety becomes less important in her life.

INTERVENTION 9

Writing a Children's Story

This intervention encourages your client to tell the story of her life in a way that would inspire a child. This means that there will be some editing involved. You probably don't want to tell a child the worst of your thoughts, the most incredible fears. But you do want to include some sense that things can be scary and that people worry. The best children's stories do.

What is the point of helping your client tell her story in this manner? She will be able to acknowledge anxieties and put them in perspective. By writing the story for a child, she will likely write in a manner that emphasizes that anxieties can be conquered, sometimes with the help of a friend.

Target skill: Using storytelling to contain and cope with anxious thoughts.

1. Check in with your client about her level of anxiety and her ability to manage her anxious thoughts. Use the scaling arrow to help your client with this. If things are better, ask how. If things are worse, ask what thoughts are driving the anxiety. Continue to emphasize that thoughts can be managed.

2. Identify today's task: writing a short children's story about an anxious thought that is managed and conquered. Explain that this can be helpful in looking at anxious thoughts as things that, although at times scary, can be dealt with and managed.

3. Review last week's homework: Look at your client's last page of the thought-record booklet. Did she add anything? Did she note any thoughts on the back? Did she share it with a friend? If she did, what did that feel like?

4. Work on today's task: You should have some paper and a stapler ready. Simple printer paper will do. If you want to, you can premake the book for your client. Take three pages of printer paper and fold them in half, then staple them in the center, like a book.

   - Provide all kinds of art materials. Your client can draw, write, glue, paint. Whatever works.

   - Begin by asking your client about a thought that makes her anxious, but not her most terrible anxious thought (because it is a children's book). Identify that thought and write it on an index card.

   - Now help your client create a story, like a fairy tale but loosely based on her life and involving this anxious thought. It's OK to include fantasy, heroes, and perhaps a villain.

   - As you talk about the story, write your client's ideas on the index cards. If your client struggles with creating a story, tell her the tale of Little Red Riding Hood (if you don't know it, look it up; it's worth it). There is anxiety and danger in that story, but in the end, justice prevails.

   - Help your client order the index cards into a story, one that she would want to tell her favorite child.

- Ask her to illustrate the story, page by page, using whatever materials she likes. Explain that children's books are not about perfection, but rather about imagination.

- If your client takes a long time illustrating each page, this is OK. You can stretch this intervention out over several sessions and explore how your client thinks about her fears using each page.

- Once the book is completed, ask her to read it to you. Compliment her on telling a story of anxieties managed and perhaps conquered.

5. Summarize what you have done today: Your client has created a children's story about her anxious thoughts. By making it a children's story she has tamed her anxious thoughts without denying them. She has shown that she can speak about them as she told you her story. If she added some elements of fantasy, she has demonstrated that it is OK to play with her story and make it what she wants it to be.

6. Assign new homework: Send the story book home with your client. Before she leaves, ask her to identify one person, perhaps a child, she could read the story to. This will be her task this week.

   If your client has trouble identifying a person, tell her that it is OK to read the story to a pet. Be sure to tell her to bring the story book back. You will need it for your next meeting.

7. Closing: Make sure your client understands the assignment and is comfortable with completing it. If she can't agree to read her story to someone, you can ask her to bring a copy of her favorite children's book to the next meeting. There will probably be something in there about anxious thoughts. Just think of *Goodnight Moon*!

INTERVENTION 10

Hearing Your Own Story

This intervention builds on the previous intervention, so you'll need the client's children's story. You will read the story to your client. There are many layers to this intervention:

- Your client hears her own story as a story. This by itself can be powerful.

- You are reading the story, thus validating your client's voice.

- It's a story of anxious thoughts and feelings and courageous mastery.

- Your client is the hero of her own story.

Target skill: Tolerating and managing anxious thoughts.

1. Begin with empathy. Check in with your client about her level of anxiety and ability to master anxious thoughts using the scaling arrow. Ask:

    Are you beginning to develop a sense of anxious thoughts as coming and going?

    When your anxious thoughts are growing, how can you relate to them in a productive way?

    When your anxious thoughts are decreasing, are you aware of it and how this happens?

2. Identify today's task: Your client will hear her own story. You will read it to her and will reflect together about the story and its impact on your client. If she wonders why you would read the story to her, tell her that is an experiment to see what listening to her own story will be like. What thoughts may come up? What does it feel like?

3. Review last week's homework: Ask your client if she read her story to anyone. If she did, what did that person say to her? How did she feel reading her own story? Did she have any anxious automatic thoughts, such as: "She will hate the story; it's not good"? And if she did, did she read the story anyway?

4. Work on today's task: Ask your client if you could have her story book for a bit. If she is reluctant to give to you, explain that you want to read her own story to her.

    - Take the story book. Hold it in a way that shows you treasure the story. Ask your client to sit back comfortably and listen. Ask if you can sit next to her so she can see the pictures in the book.

    - Explain that you will read her a children's book—her book.

- Carefully read the story with feeling. Pause so your client can see every page she has illustrated. Tell her it's OK to talk as you read it, as a child will often talk when being read a story.

- Respond to anything your client says using the story as a foundation. Use language found in the story to signal struggle, courage, and the power of realistic thinking.

- If the story contains elements of fantasy, don't skip over them. These elements may signal where your client thinks and feels she needs help.

5. Once you have concluded reading the story book, help your client reflect on the experience of hearing her own story. Ask Socratic questions like:

    - *What did you think about hearing your own story?*

    - *In what way did you love hearing your own story?*

    - *In what way were you uncomfortable with this?*

    - *Did you have any anxious thoughts about hearing your own story?*

    - *If you did have any anxious thoughts about this, can we explore together how realistic they were?*

6. It's quite possible that your client will feel a little bit like a child when you read the story to her. This is OK. If she feels awkward about this you can say: *You are not a child; you are the author of this story! It's your story.* In this manner you are reinforcing the idea that your client is the master of her own thoughts.

7. Summarize what you have done today: You have read your client's story to her and reflected on thoughts of struggle, courage, and the power of realistic thinking. Ask: *Is there anything you want to add to the story? To your experience of hearing the story?*

8. Identify new homework: Ask your client to identify one person who can read her story to her. Make sure that the person is going to be available.

    - Call this friend within the next 24 hours and schedule a visit.

    - Explain that she should ask her friend to read the story to her during the visit, just like you read the story to her. Explain that this exercise is about hearing her story from another person in another voice and honoring it.

    - Explain that it might be a nice idea to also have a cup of tea together.

    - Ask your client to explore with her friend what the experience of reading and hearing the story was like.

    - If anxious automatic thoughts about the story come up, ask your client to reflect on this with her friend and check: Are those anxious thoughts realistic?

9. Closing: Today was all about your client's story and her experience of it. Ask her if she has any questions or additional thoughts, and send her home with her story book.

INTERVENTION 11

Train of Thoughts

This intervention encourages your client to think of each anxious thought as a train. Your client can see it coming. It is very loud when it is right in front of you. It may be a freight train, meaning it will be right in front of you for a while, but it will, inevitably, pass. Such is the case with anxious thoughts, too. They can be overwhelming, but they do pass.

Target skill: Coping with anxious thoughts using metaphor.

1. Check in with your client and help her gauge her level of anxiety and her ability to manage anxious thoughts using the scaling arrow. Ask her to look back to the beginning of treatment. Is she doing things differently? If she is, what is working? Does she sometimes observe her thinking and correct her anxious thoughts?

2. Identify today's task: thinking of anxious thoughts as a passing train. Understanding that it will pass. Not jumping on the train. Many of our clients will be able to relate intuitively to the idea that anxious thoughts are like freight trains. If your client is not familiar with trains, then substitute truck for train.

3. Homework review: Ask your client if a friend read her children's story to her. How did it go? Was this a fun experience or a scary one? Or perhaps both? Did anxious automatic thoughts come up about asking her friend to do this? How did she manage these? What was her reaction to hearing her story read by a friend? Did she find this comforting?

4. Work on today's task: Ask your client to listen to you telling her a story. Explain that sometimes you will ask questions during the story. Here is the story:

   Imagine you are standing at a railroad crossing. You can hear a train coming. As it gets closer, it gets louder and louder. And as it is in front of you, it is so loud you cannot think. You see nothing but the train. You hear nothing but the train. For that moment, it seems that there is nothing but the train.

   But this is not really true. There is more than the train in this world. It just takes up all of your brain space and all of your senses. You hear the train. You see the train. You smell the train.

   Ask:

   - *In what way are anxious thoughts like a freight train?*

   - *In what way do anxious thoughts run on a track, like a freight train?*

   - *In what way do anxious thoughts run on a schedule? In what way do they not?*

   Continue with the story:

Now the freight train is passing. It is still loud. It is rattling along, but you can now see the final train car approaching. It passes you. What you see now is the back of the train. You still see it. But you don't hear it as much anymore. And you hear it less every second. Finally, the train is out of sight and out of mind. Gone.

Ask:

- *In what way are anxious thoughts like a freight train that is passing or has passed?*

- *When you don't see the freight train anymore, do you still think of it? And if you do, how much?*

- *When you are sitting at a railroad crossing in a car, waiting for the train to pass, do you get impatient?*

- *Why can it be so much harder to let go of anxious thoughts than believing that the train is really gone? Can an anxious thought be truly gone?*

- *How can you think of anxious thoughts as on a track and on a schedule? How could this be helpful?*

5. Help your client reflect on how she thinks of her anxious thoughts. Are they overwhelming for her like a freight train? When she is anxious, can she think of the metaphor of the passing train?

6. Summarize what you have done today: You have compared anxious thoughts with freight trains. You have examined how this comparison could help your client understand that anxious thoughts, while overwhelming, do pass.

7. Assign new homework: Give your client the following index card to carry with her. Ask her to take out the card when she is having an anxious and overwhelming thought and to read it out loud. Alternatively, she can also ask a friend to read the card to her.

This is just a thought.

It will pass.

I think it now, but I can let it go.

I am letting this thought go.

And if it returns, I will let it go again.

It is just a thought.

Figure 35

8. Closing: Leave your client with words of encouragement, like:

- *Not every thought that seems big is important.*
- *A thought is just a thought.*
- *It will pass.*

INTERVENTION 12

It's Not the First Thought That Counts

This intervention is designed to help your client be patient with her thoughts. Imagine this: Your client wakes up and is having a terrible anxious thought. It's the first thought that comes to her mind, just out of habit. She could jump on the freight train of the terrible anxious thought because it is there. Or she could wait and say to herself: "I just woke up. My brain is just throwing stuff out right now. This is probably not important and not relevant. Let's see what other thought comes along!"

Target skill: Sorting anxious thoughts. Assigning importance to thoughts. Coping with anxious thoughts.

1. Begin with empathy. Ask your client about her level of anxiety over the past week. You can use the scaling arrow to help her gauge her level of anxiety and ability to manage her anxious thoughts. Ask: *How did you manage your anxious thoughts? What specifically did you do?* If your client had a tough week with lots of anxious thoughts, normalize the experience. Anxious thoughts will continue to appear and, while they can be managed, they occasionally can feel overwhelming. When that happens, your client should ask others for help with thinking them through. There is no shame in asking for help!

2. Introduce today's task: learning to be patient and waiting for a better, more realistic thought. Provide education about how anxious thoughts often work. They are the first thoughts that come up, just out of habit. But this does not mean that they are of more importance than the thoughts that follow. Today your client will learn to wait, listen, and evaluate!

3. Review last week's homework: Ask your client if she still has the index card you gave her during your last meeting. Did she use it? And if she did, was it helpful? Can she give you an example? If she did not use it, find out why. What stood in the way? Did she lose it? If so, just make another one. Explain that you are trying to give her as many strategies as possible for managing anxious thoughts. What has worked well for her? What has not? It's OK not to use the tools that are not working well. Which tools will she use instead?

4. Work on today's task: Learning to be patient and waiting for a better, more realistic and less anxious thought. You can use the following image to help illustrate the task:

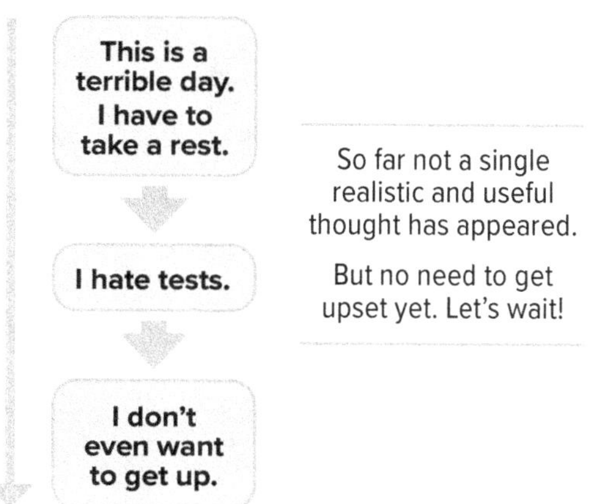

Figure 36

5. Ask your client if she ever has these kinds of start to her day. Ask:

   - *How easy is it to just give up?*

   - *What do you tell yourself in response to the anxious thought that makes you want to give up?*

   - *What would it be like to simply let those thoughts happen?*

   - *Could it be possible to simply let the anxious thoughts be, not making them bigger, but also not denying them?*

6. Eventually a realistic and useful thought will come along. She just has to recognize it. Perhaps something like this:

Figure 37

7. Ask your client:

    - *What is different about this thought?*

    - *Would you be able to recognize that this thought is different?*

    - *How would being less emotional about an anxious thought make it easier to recognize the realistic and useful thought?*

8. Ask your client to create a "chain of thoughts" today, listing each anxious thought until she gets to a realistic and useful one. While she is doing so, you can help her explore how she responds to each. Is she adding to the anxiousness of the thought? Or is she simply recognizing the thought, then moving to the next one?

9. Summarize what you have done so far. You have looked at how anxious thoughts come about out of habit. You have asked your client to be patient and wait for a realistic and useful thought. When that thought appeared, you encouraged your client to spend time with it.

10. Assign homework: Give your client a set of at least seven printed frames for those useful and realistic thoughts. (You can find a set of frames to copy in the appendix.)

    Ask her to begin every day listening for her thoughts, acknowledging anxious ones, but not spending too much time with them. When the valuable and realistic thought comes along, she should write it down in a frame. Give her as many frames as she needs. She will learn that she has the capacity to think useful and realistic thoughts more often than not.

    Also, give your client an envelope to collect those thoughts, and have her bring the envelope to her next meeting with you.

11. Closing: Check in with your client. Ask: *Are you able to recognize and value your realistic and useful thoughts?* Explain that this will take practice. It does not come naturally, but the realistic and useful thoughts are there. We just need to give them time.

No Food For Anxious Thoughts

This intervention encourages your client to think of anxiety as something that needs to "feed" on anxious thoughts. The more your client feeds her anxious thoughts, the bigger they get.

Target skill: Relating to anxious thoughts in a meaningful way. Coping.

1. Check in with your client. Use the scaling arrow to help your client gauge her anxiety level and her ability to manage anxious thoughts. Did any anxious thoughts stand out this week? What were they? What about other thoughts? Did any thoughts that made her feel happy or accomplished stand out? What were those about?

    - Help your client recognize that while she has anxious thoughts, she also has other thoughts that she can focus on.

2. Identify today's task: Learning to relate to anxious thoughts in a meaningful way. Explain that:

    - An anxious thought can just be there.

    - She can relate to it in many ways.

    - One of the ways she can relate to it is to believe the message that the anxious thought sends.

    - There are other ways of relating to the anxious thought.

    - It can just "sit" there.

    - The anxious thought can scream at her and demand attention.

    - She does not have to give it attention.

3. Review last week's homework: Ask your client to take out the envelope containing valuable and realistic thoughts. Ask your client to read each thought to you, and help her explore why each is valuable and realistic. Ask:

    - *What situation does this thought relate to?*

    - *How did it help you or make the situation better?*

    If your client has only one or two thoughts in her envelope, this is OK. Just spend more time on those.

4. Work on today's task. Ask your client to name a particularly pesky anxious thought. Then show your client the following drawing:

Figure 39

5. Ask your client to think of her anxiety as that hungry mouth. It just demands to be fed. Now, ask your client to come up with two kinds of thoughts in response to the anxious thought. You can use this chart to help:

Particularly Pesky Anxious Thought
Thoughts that feed anxiety:
Thoughts that don't feed anxiety:

Figure 40

- Help your client recognize that thoughts that feed anxiety are usually unrealistic and faulty, and thoughts that don't feed anxiety are usually realistic and valuable.

- If necessary, you can always go back to evaluating the evidence for and against the anxious thought using this chart:

Automatic Thought	Evidence for AT	Evidence against AT

Figure 41

6. Go back to the image of the mouth.

Figure 42

Ask your client to talk to the image, beginning with the words:

I am not going to feed you. You can close your mouth. Here is what I have to say:

Figure 43

Have your client enter her thoughts that do not feed anxiety. Make sure that there are plenty of them. Help if you need to, but don't tell your client what to think in response to the anxious thought that wants to be fed. Ask Socratic questions to elicit helpful thoughts your client may have.

7. Summarize what you have done so far: You have imagined anxiety as a big hungry mouth that demands to be fed. You have identified helpful and realistic thoughts in response. That would look like this:

Figure 44

8. Identify homework: Give your client at least seven talk-bubble pages like this:

Figure 45

Ask her to write down any helpful and realistic thoughts she has in response to the particularly pesky anxious thought. Explain that this will help her build a library of responses. Give her an envelope to collect her thoughts. Ask her to bring this envelope to the next meeting.

9. Closing: Explain again that today you have worked together on not feeding anxious thoughts. Ask your client to consider the possibility that she can talk back to and silence the big mouth. If your client has any questions about the assignment, answer them now.

INTERVENTION 14

Losing Your Marbles

This intervention plays with the phrase "I am losing my marbles," which is often used to describe a state of feeling out of control. In this intervention, anxious and unrealistic thoughts are the marbles, the kind of thoughts that you can and should lose.

Target skill: Coping with anxious thoughts using metaphor. Relating to anxious thoughts differently.

1. Check in with your client and ask how the past few days went. Help your client gauge her level of anxiety and ability to manage anxious thoughts using the scaling arrow. If your client's level of anxiety is not decreasing, focus on her ability to manage those anxious thoughts. When has she been successful with this and lived her life in spite of her anxiety?

2. Identify today's task: thinking of anxious and unrealistic thoughts as marbles. You can roll them. You can collect them. They can bump into each other. Ask: *Have you ever heard the phrase "I am afraid to lose my marbles"? In this case that would be OK because if your anxious thoughts are your marbles, you may occasionally want to lose them.*

3. Review last week's homework: Ask your client to take out the envelope containing her helpful and realistic thoughts. Review them with her. Ask about the situations in which these thoughts appeared and how they worked out. You can suggest that your client continue cataloging more of her helpful thoughts and put them in the envelope. Explain that she can then draw from the envelope when anxious thoughts overwhelm her.

4. Work on today's task: Today you are going to roll marbles. Each marble will represent an anxious and unreasonable thought.

5. Show your client the bowl full of marbles. Say: Each of these marbles represents an anxious and unreasonable thought. Your job is to roll each one of them as far away as you can or want to. You can start with a really big marble, if you want to. One of those would represent a particularly pesky anxious thought. Before you roll it away, name the thought, then say: "And I am letting you go." You can give your client the following example of how she can send off her anxious thought:

    > *This big fat marble stands for my anxious thought about messing up. The anxious thought tells me: Everything you do, you mess it up. You know what, anxious thought? I am letting you go.*

6. Ask your client to roll away her anxious thoughts one by one. While she is doing this, help her reflect on them and her ability to let them go.

7. If your client says: "But look, they are still there," this is a great opening for a conversation about the nature of anxious thoughts. Yes, they are still there, but they are a bit farther away.

Anxious thoughts do not just disappear. The brain will continue to produce them, but this does not mean that your client has to hold them close! It's OK to be playful with them and to roll them away. It might even be fun to dump the whole bowl of anxious-thought marbles and roll them all at once.

8.　Summarize what you have done today: You have asked your client to "lose her marbles" by rolling away her anxious thoughts one by one. You have reflected on the nature of anxious thoughts. They do not just go away, but you can distance yourself from them.

9.　Assign homework: Let your client pick out a marble. Ask her to roll that marble away from her every time she has a particularly pesky anxious thought, if possible. When the thought comes to mind, tell her to say, "There you are, you pesky anxious thought. I am letting you go."

10.　Closing: Today you have identified another way of letting go of anxious thoughts and reflected on the fact that they do not completely disappear. Ask your client if she has any questions about how anxious thoughts work, then send her home with her marble.

INTERVENTION 15

Unwrapping It and Wrapping It Up

This intervention encourages your client to think of thoughts as little (or big) packages. They are there, sitting right in front of her. She can open them—or not! There is such a thing as an unwanted present or a present that is just not right. Those presents can be wrapped back up and put away or passed on.

Target skill: Relating to and coping with anxious thoughts. Examining anxious thoughts.

1. Check in with your client about her level of anxiety and ability to manage anxious thoughts using the scaling arrow. How well is your client able to manage those pesky thoughts? What method is she using to manage them? Who has she enlisted to help her when she needs help?

2. Identify today's task: Thinking of anxious thoughts as packages that can be opened or not. They can even be returned to sender!

3. Review last week's homework: Ask your client if she used the marble to "roll away" her anxious thoughts. When she rolled the marble, did she use the script for letting the thought go? Was this fun? Or did she feel silly?

4. Work on today's task: Ask your client to imagine that a stack of packages has arrived at her door. Something like this:

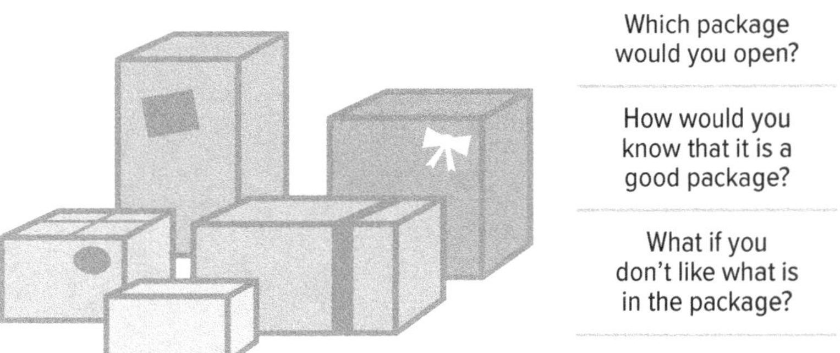

Figure 46

5. Ask your client to describe packages or gifts she has received that she did not like or that were not right for her.

6. Then ask her if it is OK to not like a package or a gift. Help her reflect on her feelings about evaluating a present to see if it fits into her life.

7. Show your client the following picture:

Figure 47

Ask: *Would she want to open this package? It looks good!*

8. Now ask your client to imagine this: *What if the package looks good, but here is what is inside:*

Figure 48

Say: *It's just a bunch of anxious thoughts packaged to look good and feel important.*

9. Ask your client what she would do with a package that contains junk thoughts. Here are some options:

   - Return to sender.
   - Put it into the trash.
   - Smash the box.
   - Put the junk thoughts back in the box and wait until you need kindling for lighting a fire.

10. Remind your client that junk (anxious) thoughts are like a big fancy-looking package that you want to open. Say: *It's OK to put everything back in the box. It's OK to throw it out or return it to sender. If you don't like what is in it, you don't have to accept it!*

11. Help your client make the connection between "junk packages" and pesky anxious thoughts.

12. Summarize what you have done today: You have explored opening packages. While some packages may look good, they may actually contain junk,

like thoughts that are unrealistic and unhelpful. There is no need to keep junk in your house, or in your brain!

13. Assign new homework: Give your client a small origami paper box (or any other small box). Ask her to collect her junk (anxious) thoughts in that box by writing them on small pieces of paper. At the end of the week, she can do with them whatever she wants:

    - Dump them in the trash.
    - Bring them into your session to talk about them.
    - Use them for kindling.
    - Stomp on them.
    - Talk to them.
    - Tell them how wrong they are.
    - And so much more . . .

14. Closing: Send your client off with the following thought: She can decide what to do with an anxious pesky thought. Just because it is there does not mean it is true!

Behavioral Interventions for Anxiety Disorders

What is the core of behavioral interventions of anxiety disorders? What are we asking our clients to do and why? In many ways the term *exposure* is the answer. You will be asking your client to engage in behaviors and actions that are anxiety pro-voking *in spite of their anxiety*. This is where behavioral and cognitive interventions intersect.

There will never be a way for your client to understand that anxiety can be managed if she does not expose herself to anxiety-provoking behaviors. If your client is anxious about going to school, the cure for this anxiety does not lie in staying at home, but rather in going to school. However, if your client has a tremendous amount of anxiety about going to school, forcing her to go (in essence, "dragging" her to school) will only make things worse. **The key is to incrementally expose your client to anxiety-provoking behaviors and situations, step by step.**

If your client avoids all anxiety-inducing behaviors and situations, she can never learn that she can manage her anxiety. If she puts herself in an overwhelming situa-tion, she may move into an involuntary neurobiological fight/flight/freeze response. When your client is in a fight/flight/freeze mode, her body and brain focus on per-ceived threats to the exclusion of all else and she cannot learn.

The key is to expose your client to behaviors that induce "just enough" anxiety. This means that your client is definitely out of her comfort zone (she feels anxiety), but not in an overwhelming way that shuts down her ability to think and learn. Here is how you can illustrate this for your client:

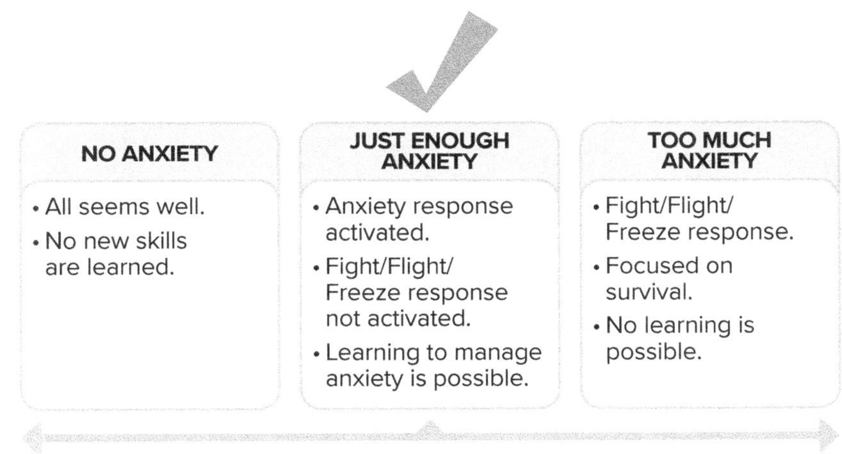

Figure 49

For high-functioning clients, it may be possible to "live through" overwhelming anxiety and learn from the experience. We do not recommend "flooding" your client with anxiety because many of our clients have co-occurring conditions such as substance abuse or posttraumatic stress disorder (PTSD).

If your client is struggling with an anxiety disorder and substance abuse, and she is flooded with more anxiety than she can handle, she may be in danger of using a substance.

If your client is struggling with PTSD and another anxiety disorder, she may be in danger of a dissociative episode and lose her ability to manage intense affect.

Again, the key is to help your client learn to gradually widen her window of tolerance. Take the example of your client who is very anxious about going to school. Here is what you could do:

- On day one, you and your client drive by the school and look at the building.

- On day two, you park the car in the parking lot and look at the building.

- On day three, you and your client get out of the car and walk to the entrance.

- On day four, you and your client walk into school and into the guidance office.

- And so forth . . .

It is important to accurately gauge your client's baseline level of anxiety. If she is moderately anxious, you could start with entering the building together rather than just driving by.

If you are going to expose your client to behaviors and situations that make her anxious, it is of vital importance that she has the skills to manage her increasing anxiety. That is why behavioral interventions for anxiety begin with skill building.

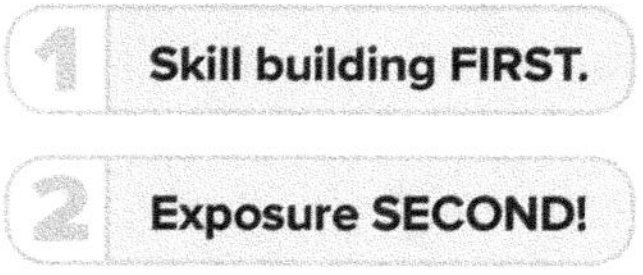

Figure 50

INTERVENTION 16

Skill Building: Breathe Through It

Target skill: Anxiety-coping using breath.

1. Welcome your client. Check in with her about her level of anxiety and ability to manage it. How anxious is she today? What is she anxious about today? Get to know that "flavor" of your client's anxiety.

2. Introduce today's task: learning to "breathe through" anxiety. Explain that this means slowing down her breath to avoid hyperventilating. If your client does not know what hyperventilating is, you may want to demonstrate. Also, explain that our brains do not work very well when we hyperventilate.

3. Work on today's task: Begin with education. Tell your client that:

   - anxiety often begins with breathing too fast (hyperventilation);

   - slowing down breath can help regulate the body's anxiety response; and

   - breathing slowly is not meant to avoid anxiety-provoking behaviors/actions/situation, but rather to manage the anxiety that arises.

4. Demonstrate calm breathing. You can use the "smell the soup, blow on the soup" metaphor. Say this:

   Imagine that there is a bowl of soup in front of you. It smells good. Put your nose close to the bowl and inhale deeply, counting to three.

   Then, breathe out through your mouth, blowing on the soup slowly, counting to ten.

   Demonstrate at least three times. It is important to breathe out longer than breathing in, but not so long that it becomes uncomfortable. Your client should not be gasping for air when she is done.

5. Now practice this with your client. Say: *Let's do this together. It will take a while to become comfortable with this. Don't worry about doing this perfectly right now; just give it a try.* Practice at least three breaths with your client.

6. Then ask: *What was this like? What was comfortable? What was not?*

7. If necessary, demonstrate and practice together again. If it helps your client, you can put on some relaxation music.

8. Some of our clients are anxious about their bodies or their breath. If your client feels more anxious when learning to slow her breath, start with simply sitting together and listening to some soothing music. Slow and soothing music can also help slow down breath. You can then introduce the idea of consciously slowing down breath.

9. Summarize what you have done today: You have learned that anxiety starts in the body, and that slowing down our breathing can calm the body's anxiety response. You have learned and practiced how to slow down breath.

10. Assign homework: Ask your client to begin and end each day with three consciously slowed-down breaths. Also explain that there is no need to worry about perfection. Ask your client to simply try this without worry. If it helps your client, she may want to end her practice saying:

    I can do this. I can get through this.

11. Closing: Once again explain that anxiety lives in the body and that there are ways to help the body decrease an anxiety response. Check in with your client and answer any questions she may have.

INTERVENTION 17

Behavior Baseline

Before you can change anxious behaviors and actions, you need to know what they are. What is your client avoiding? What is she doing because of her anxiety? What is she not doing because of her anxiety?

Target skill: Activity monitoring to decrease avoidance behaviors. Establishing baseline for avoidance behaviors.

1. Check in with your client. What went well over the last week? Use the scaling arrow to help your client gauge her level of anxiety.

2. Identify today's task: learning to monitor activities related to anxiety such as avoidance behaviors. Explain that avoidance behaviors are things we do in order to avoid doing other things that cause us to experience anxiety such as:

   - watching TV to avoid writing an essay,

   - surfing the Internet to avoid talking to a partner, and

   - staying in bed to avoid the boss at work.

3. Review last week's homework: Ask your client if she practiced her calm breathing. If she did, what did it feel like? Was it difficult? How so? Was she able to practice in the morning and in the evening? Which seemed a better time to practice? Suggest to your client that she establish a time at least once a day to practice calm breathing so it can become second nature.

4. Work on today's task: learning to monitor anxious avoidance. Here is a chart that might be helpful:

Things I avoid because they make me feel anxious	Things I do to avoid the thing I am anxious about	How much time I spend avoiding the things that make me anxious

Figure 51

5. Help your client complete the chart by asking Socratic questions about things she avoids doing. Communicate clearly that there will be no shaming about avoidance activities. You are just trying to establish a baseline. It is not necessary to list all of your client's avoidance behaviors. Once you have three, help your client rank them by order of importance.

   How do you know what is important?

   - If it's unsafe, it is important (example: avoids eating).

   - If it takes up a lot of time, it is important.

   - If it destabilizes your client's life, it is important (example: not going to work).

6. Once the chart is completed, help your client reflect on what she sees. Stress that you are using a scientific method (establishing baseline) to solve a problem.

7. Now: List the three most important behaviors or activities your client avoids because of her anxiety.

   Write them out on an index card like this:
   1. Going to the doctor.
   2. Looking at the mail.
   3. Cleaning the house.

8. Ask your client what it feels like to see those things in writing. What if they became her goals? Does this question trigger anxiety?

9. If it does, practice calm breathing together.

10. Summarize what you have done today: You have learned about and charted avoidance behaviors. You have ranked them in order of importance, and you have thought about turning them into goals. You have also used calm breathing to help your client manage anxiety about her avoidance behaviors.

11. Identify new homework: Ask your client to continue to monitor her avoidance behaviors over the next few days using the chart. Send home at least one additional blank copy for your client and ask her to bring it to the next meeting.

12. Closing: Explain that you are not trying to eliminate anxiety, but rather help her learn to manage the behavioral response (avoidance) to anxiety. Ask if she has any questions about activity monitoring and avoidance behaviors.

INTERVENTION 18

Skill Building: Opening the Senses, Opening the Mind

This intervention builds on the first mindfulness intervention, which focused on helping your client learn and practice calm breathing. In order to learn this, your client had to become more aware of her breath and her ability to slow it down.

Mindfulness is the full immersion in what you are doing. You are aware of what you are doing, and you are observing what you are doing nonjudgmentally.

So, what is mindful breathing? It's breathing with an awareness of the act of breathing.

What is mindful eating? It's eating with an awareness of the act of eating.

Mindfulness requires openness to sensory experiences and to everything the mind may bring your way.

Target skill: Anxiety-coping through mindfulness.

1. Begin with breathing. Ask your client to take three deep and calm breaths with you. It may be a good idea to demonstrate this again to set the tone. Then breathe together.

2. Welcome your client. Help her gauge her level of anxiety and her ability to manage it over the past few weeks using the scaling arrow. What went well? What were her most difficult and anxious experiences? Help your client be nonjudgmental about her difficulties. Encourage her to just be aware of them but in a nonjudgmental way.

3. Identify today's task: becoming more mindful and opening the senses. Explain that this involves taking in all kinds of experiences without resistance and judgment. What does it mean to take things in without judgment? Here is an example:

   Your client is learning to practice calm breathing. While she is working on this, a fly lands on her arm. She notices it and swats the fly, then immediately feels guilty about not staying on task and interrupting her breathing practice.

   A mindful approach to the dilemma of the fly would be to simply notice the distraction, deal with it, and then go back to practicing the calm breathing. Things happen. Such is life. No need to judge oneself.

4. Review last week's homework: Look at the avoidance chart your client has brought. Has she added any new behaviors that she avoids due to anxiety? Ask her to tally how much time she spends avoiding anxiety-inducing behaviors and activities. Wonder out loud: *What would you be able to do with all the time spent avoiding anxiety-inducing activities?*

5. Work on today's task: becoming mindful and opening the senses.

   - Ask your client to look around and describe what she sees in as much detail as she can. Remind her that this is not a competition about noticing detail, but an exercise.

- Listen attentively and comment as appropriate.

- Ask your client to listen and to describe all the sounds that she is hearing in as much detail as she can.

- Listen attentively and comment as appropriate.

- Now, ask your client to talk about her anxiety-provoking activity/ behavior in the same manner. She should simply observe her thoughts, notice and describe her thoughts and feelings and the activity that she is trying to avoid.

- Listen attentively and comment as appropriate. If your client becomes judgmental of herself while she is talking, simply help her notice this. Don't judge her for judging herself. If your client becomes anxious, ask her to notice that, too.

6. Once you have completed this exercise, help your client reflect on the sim- ilarities between the sights and sounds she described and the anxiety-pro- voking behaviors/activities she described. These are all just things that exist. Help her understand that she can observe her thoughts and behaviors like any other thing.

7. Explore with your client how she can use mindful immersion in what is around her as a way to calm herself in the face of anxiety. Explain that mindful immersion is not meant to avoid anxiety. On the contrary, it is meant to assist with being fully present in any experience no matter how pleasant or unpleasant.

8. Summarize what you have done today: You have worked on understanding mindfulness and mindful immersion in experience. You have applied this idea to sensory experiences such as sight and sound. And you have learned that mindful immersion and observation can also apply to observing one's own mindful avoidance, without judgment.

9. Identify new homework: Ask your client to set aside two minutes (or more) every morning before she begins her day to mindfully immerse herself in all that is around her. What does she see? What does she hear? What does she taste and smell? If she notices anxiety passing through her, she should notice that, too.

10. Closing: Today was all about mindfulness. Ask your client to come up with her own definition of mindfulness. If there is anything to clarify, clarify it now. Take notes and save those notes for your next session.

INTERVENTION 19

Skill Building: Move Through It

Target skill: Anxiety-coping using the body.

1. Begin with a breath. Ask your client to calmly take three breaths with you. You may want to demonstrate again. Emphasize that perfection is not important and that practice will help with mastery of this skill.

2. Check in with your client: Use the scaling arrow to help her gauge her level of anxiety and ability to manage anxious thoughts and behaviors. What went well over the past week? What was your client anxious about but did anyway? How did that experience go? Did she feel like she accomplished something? Or was she overwhelmed? Explain that both of those feelings are normal responses to anxiety-provoking thoughts and behaviors. If your client did something in spite of her anxiety, find out how this came about. How did she work through her anxiety? Perhaps she just ignored it. How did that work?

3. Identify today's task: using motion (in this case, the act of walking) as a backdrop for talking about anxiety-provoking actions/behaviors/events. Explain that walking may help with regulating the body's anxiety response.

4. Review last week's homework: Look at the avoidance behavior chart your client brought in. Is there anything new and important on the chart? If there is, is your client ready to make this a goal? If your client did not complete the homework, ask her if she feels like she is avoiding it. If she is, normalize that behavior. A lot of people avoid things all the time. But explain that in order to address avoidance, you are going to need the right kind of data—a record of what your client is avoiding and how. Ask if she can try again.

5. Work on today's task: "moving through" anxiety-provoking behaviors. Ask your client to pick one activity from the list of behaviors she is avoiding. Explain that you are going to "expose" her to the topic of the behavior by talking about it together. Say:

   - *I will not ask you to engage in that behavior today.*

   - *But we will talk about the behavior.*

   - *This will help you get used to the thought of the behavior.*

   - *If you feel anxious about this, this is OK. We will gauge your level of anxiety frequently. If you become overwhelmingly anxious, let me know.*

   Reassure your client that in the event she becomes too anxious, you will take a break and help her regulate using calm breathing.

6. Explain that you will be walking together while talking. If you are in a small room, you may have to walk in a small circle. Explain that being in motion can help her regulate her anxiety without avoiding it.

7. Begin walking together. Ask your client questions about the behavior she is avoiding. Here are some sample questions:

   - *What happens when you . . . ?*

   - *When is the last time that you . . . ?*

   - *Who is usually with you when you . . . ?*

   - *What is the worst thing that could happen when you . . . ?*

   - *What is the best thing that could happen when you . . . ?*

8. Pay attention to your client's body language. If she seems overwhelmed by anxiety, take a break. Use the scaling arrow to determine together how anxious your client is. If she rates her anxiety at seven or higher, take a break and practice calm breathing together until her anxiety level is below seven.

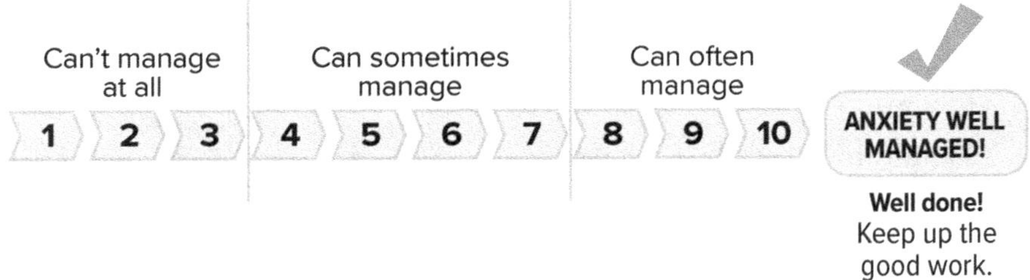

Figure 52

9. Once your client's anxiety is managed, be sure to move back into the activity of walking and talking about the anxiety-provoking behavior. Go back to asking questions about the behavior until it becomes normal to talk about it. Your client is now beginning to habituate to talking about the anxiety-provoking behavior.

10. Compliment your client on a job well done. Explain that today you have worked together on tolerating talking about the anxiety-provoking behavior in preparation for engaging in it. Explain that, like breathing, walking while talking can be helpful to regulate the body's anxiety response.

11. Be sure to explain that running while talking does not work because this would increase your client's heart rate and rate of breathing.

12. Assign homework: Ask your client to pick a friend and talk with him or her about the anxiety-provoking behavior that she generally avoids. Suggest that the two of them go for a walk together while talking to help regulate your client's anxiety.

13. Be sure to explain that your client should not pick the most anxiety-provoking behavior. This could cause her to feel overwhelmed, which would only reinforce her anxiety.

14. Closing: Summarize again that today was about learning to talk about anxiety-provoking behaviors while moving the body to regulate anxiety. See if your client has any questions. If she does, answer them.

INTERVENTION 20

Skill Building: Change the Scenery

This intervention is designed to help your client change her state of mind when she is anxious about an action, behavior, or event. Anxiety feeds itself, and every anxious thought seems to call for another one. We can interrupt the cycle using a sensory experience—in this case, an image. The sensory experience is not meant to aid in avoidance of an anxiety-inducing action, behavior, or event, but to calm the body's stress response.

Target skill: Anxiety-coping using visual input.

1. Begin with breathing. Welcome your client and ask her to take three calm breaths with you. Take it slow. Pay attention to your client's comfort or discomfort with this. If there is a need, explain again how to slow breath using the "smell the soup, blow on the soup" metaphor.

2. Check in with your client. What went well over the past week? What was she able to do in spite of her anxiety? Did she go to school? Did she give a presentation? Compliment your client on a job well done. Explain that you understand how difficult it can be to live with anxiety and that you know how hard she is working.

3. Introduce today's task: changing the scenery when anxiety about an upcoming behavior, action, or event is threatening to take over and lead to avoidance. You can give an example like this:

   > *Perhaps you have arranged to go on a date. You really want to go, but your anxiety kicks in just as you are about to leave. Your anxiety tells you that you should not go, and your anxious thoughts kick in full force, one after another. Your body's stress response is making things more difficult.*

   This is the time when your client should change the scenery by looking at a beloved or delightful image.

4. Review last week's homework: Ask your client if she was able to discuss her anxiety- provoking action or behavior with a friend while walking together. Did walking help soothe the anxiety? What was her friend's response? How did she feel after walking and talking with her friend? Does she think the experience may be worth repeating?

5. Work on today's task: changing the scenery when anxiety takes over there is a danger she may avoid an upcoming behavior, event, or action because of her anxiety.

   - Explain that changing the scenery is different than avoidance. It simply resets her body from a stress response to a calmer state. Then you can go back to what you were going to do.

   - Ask your client to name a place, person, image, or experience that always gives her a sense of calm. Here are some examples:

- a puppy
- a beautiful lake
- a smiling baby
- flowers
- a family picture

6. Be sure to spend enough time to figure out what truly gives your client a sense of calm. Pay close attention to her body language and facial expressions while she talks about choosing her calming image. When you see your client's face and body settle, you are probably on the right track. Keep in mind that what calms a person can be very specific.

7. Stay away from using video gaming to create a sense of calm. Your client is not truly calm when she is gaming. In most cases, gaming numbs rather than awakens one to the beauty of life.

8. Spend some time looking for an image of your client's calming prompt. Perhaps she already has the perfect photograph with her. There are many beautiful images you can find on the Internet. Just search for "cute animals" and you will find a multitude of images that should make you and your client smile.

9. Look at the image together. Ask your client to describe it to you. What kind of feeling does she get when she looks at it? Help your client fully immerse herself in the image!

10. If you can, print out the image or help your client find an easy way to access it on her phone by writing down the web address.

11. Take out an index card and either glue the image on the card or write the web address for the image on the card.

12. Review what you have done today: Your client has learned to change the scenery in preparation for engaging in an anxiety-provoking behavior. Explain again that changing the scenery can help reset the body's stress response system. This, in turn, will help her engage in the activity.

13. Assign homework: Give your client the index card with the calming image or web address. Ask her to carry it with her and look at it for a minute at the beginning of every day. She should then carry it with her and take it out when anxiety about a behavior or action threatens to take over. Ask her to fully immerse herself in the image for a minute or two, then return to her task at hand. Of course, she can repeat use of the calming image as needed, and perhaps the image will embed itself in her memory after a while and just be with her wherever she goes.

14. Closing: Ask your client if she has any questions. If she does, answer them. Wish her well on her journey of learning to calm her mind and body's stress response.

INTERVENTION 21

Leaning into Discomfort

This intervention introduces the idea of beginning with exposure to anxiety-provoking behaviors. Your client will learn to question the assumption that avoiding anxiety-provoking behaviors will eliminate her anxiety and hence make her feel better. Your client will learn to look at anxiety about a behavior or action as a signal that she has an opportunity to grow.

Target skill: Understanding exposure to anxiety-provoking behaviors. Insight.

1. Begin with breathing. Welcome your client and ask her to take three calm breaths with you. Take it slow. Pay attention to your client's comfort or discomfort with this. If there is a need, explain again how to slow the breath using the "smell the soup, blow on the soup" metaphor.

2. Identify today's task: curiously leaning into discomfort. You should explain that this means:

    - not running away from anxiety-provoking behaviors, situations, or events.

    - asking: What am I missing if I run away now?

    - asking: Is this an opportunity to learn and grow?

    - acknowledging anxiety but not the limits it imposes.

    If your client thinks this is crazy, ask her why. Then give examples of things that she may have learned that seemed impossible and crazy, such as:

    - learning to swim. Swimming is a crazy idea. It seems truly impossible that we should be able to stay afloat!

    - riding a bicycle. Surely, we would fall over.

    - getting on an airplane.

    All of the examples contain a variety of metaphors that can be used for introducing the idea of curiously leaning into discomfort. Here is how this works for swimming:

    - When you learn how to swim, you will probably be afraid.

    - You will probably swallow some water.

    - You will probably get very tired.

    - But once you know how to swim, it can be so much fun. It is worth it.

3. Review last week's homework: changing the scenery by looking at a calming image. Ask your client if she has used her index card over the past week. Was she able to begin each day with the image? How did this impact her? Did she use the image when she became anxious? Was she able to return to her activities once she was calm?

    Did the calming image come to her mind unintentionally? If it did, this would be a great thing, as it is becoming part of her emotional vocabulary.

4. Work on today's task: curiously leaning into discomfort.

    - Begin by asking your client to identify a behavior or activity she would
      like to engage in, but avoids, because it would make her anxious. Ask
      her to write or draw the activity in this box.

Figure 53

5. Now: Change the frame just a little bit. Here is the new frame:

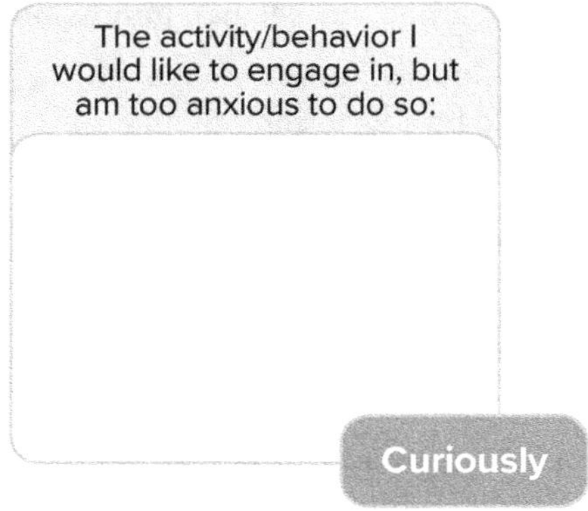

Figure 54

Ask your client to write or draw the activity again in this box. Then ask:

- *What changes if you become curious about the activity?*
- *How can curiosity help you lean into discomfort about the anticipated anxiety?*
- *Is there a payoff for leaning into discomfort?*
- *What will you gain if you engage in the behavior?*

If this is helpful, ask your client to give a detailed description of the activity she would like to engage in. What would it feel like to roller blade, go on a date, go on a trip, etc.?

6. Ask your client what she would need to curiously approach the activity she would like to engage in.

   - Would it help to be calmer? How can this happen?
   - Would it help to know more about how anxiety works? What information is needed?
   - Would it help to have a support person present? Who would this be?
   - Would it help to make a plan how to make it through? What needs to be on the plan?

7. Help your client reflect on her curiosity. Encourage her to view it as a friend. You can say things like:

   - *Curiosity can open doors.*
   - *Curiosity helps you learn new things.*
   - *Curiosity makes your life bigger and better.*

8. Summarize what you have done together today: You have explored the role of curiosity as a helper and a friend. You have explored how curiosity can balance out anxiety about a behavior or activity.

9. Assign new homework: Give your client the curiosity frame to take home. Ask her to meet with or talk with a friend on the phone and discuss her curiosity about the activity. While talking, ask her to make a note of her feelings on the back of the frame. Also ask her to note her friend's responses. Was her friend supportive or anxious?

10. Closing: Before your client goes home, ask her to adopt a curious stance about an item in the room. What questions would she like to ask her item? Here is an example of what this may look like for a plant:

    - *Where did you come from?*
    - *Are you happy here?*
    - *Do you see me?*
    - *Would you like some water?*

Help your client practice curiosity!

INTERVENTION 22

Facing Anxiety: Beginning Exposure

Your client has now learned (and hopefully mastered) basic skills for calming her mind and body. Keep in mind that moving into exposure to higher levels of anxiety will only work if your client has learned and practiced her calming skills. She needs to be somewhat comfortable with using calming skills, and they should eventually become second nature.

While learning and practicing calming skills, your client has also been exposed to thoughts about anxiety-provoking behaviors. CBT calls this *introspective exposure* (as opposed to real-life, *in vivo* exposure). Keep in mind that exposure should raise your client's anxiety somewhat, but not so much that she becomes overwhelmed and moves into a fight/flight/freeze response, in which case she would be unable to learn anxiety-management skills.

Target skill: Tolerating exposure to anxiety-provoking behaviors.

1. Begin with breathing. Ask your client to take three calm breaths with you. Take it slow. When you are done, explore with your client how comfortable she has become with using breath to calm herself. Ask:

    - *Is this becoming second nature?*

    - *Do you practice calm breathing every day?* (If she does not, encourage her to do so at the beginning and end of every day.)

2. Introduce today's task: beginning real exposure to . . .

    Explain that in order to manage anxiety, it will be necessary to engage in a real anxiety-provoking behavior or activity. You may want to go back to the behavior baseline chart (Intervention 2). What behaviors does your client avoid? Which behavior or activity is she willing to try?

3. Review last week's homework. Ask who your client met with to explore the curiosity frame. What was the other person's response? How did it feel to express curiosity in spite of anxiety?

4. Work on today's task. Ask your client to rate the behaviors listed on the behavior baseline chart on a scale from 1-3, with one being a little anxiety provoking and 3 being very anxiety provoking.

5. Once she has done so, ask her to pick a behavior rated 1. You can explain that, to be successful, it is best to begin with a behavior that evokes some anxiety, but not too much.

6. Once she has chosen a behavior or activity, help your client make a plan for engaging in it. The plan could look something like this:

Anxiety Provoking Behavior		
When I will engage in this behavior:	Day:	Time
What I will do if my anxiety level goes up:		
1.		
2.		
3.		
4.		

Figure 55

7. Your client should pick specific and workable skills to manage her anxiety. These are skills she is comfortable with and that have become close to second nature.

8. Make a contingency plan: Let's pretend that your client engages in the anxiety-provoking behavior and goes through all of the coping skills, but none of them seem to work. What should your client do then?

   - Return to the idea of mindful immersion. Explain that it is possible to observe and experience anxiety without "running with it." Ask your client to just let the anxiety be. It comes, but it also goes. Your client should, if at all possible, go through with the planned anxiety-provoking experience because this is the only way she can learn that anxiety can be managed.

   - If your client cannot succeed by herself, she may need to be coached through the experience. Sometimes it may be necessary for you to accompany your client into the community and walk her through the process of engaging in an anxiety-provoking behavior. If this is necessary, talk with your supervisor and make a plan that ensures everyone's confidentiality as much as possible.

   - There are situations in which your client may need to enlist a friend as a coach. Clearly, if going out on a date is an anxiety-provoking behavior, you cannot go with your client, and you should talk about who might be able to coach her through the experience.

9. Summarize what you have done today: You have made a plan for your client to engage in an anxiety-provoking behavior in real life. You have also chosen calming/coping skills your client can use to make it through.

10. Assign new homework: You know what is coming. Your client will engage in the anxiety-provoking behavior in real life. Ask her to take a few notes about how it went and bring those notes to your next meeting.

11. Closing: Send your client home with a few words of support. Say something like:

> *You have come a long way, and it is time to put those skills you have learned into practice. You can do this. You can* [the anxiety provoking behavior your client will engage in, in spite of being anxious about it], *even if it causes you to be anxious. You can manage this.*

INTERVENTION 23

Facing Anxiety: Stepping Up Exposure

Your client should move on to this intervention if she has successfully engaged in the last intervention. If your client did not complete her homework, you should continue to work on completing the exposure intervention until she does. Your client needs the experience of successfully completing a behavior in spite of anxiety.

What does success mean? Success means that your client was able to manage her anxiety. It does not mean that your client did not become anxious. Here is what success looks like:

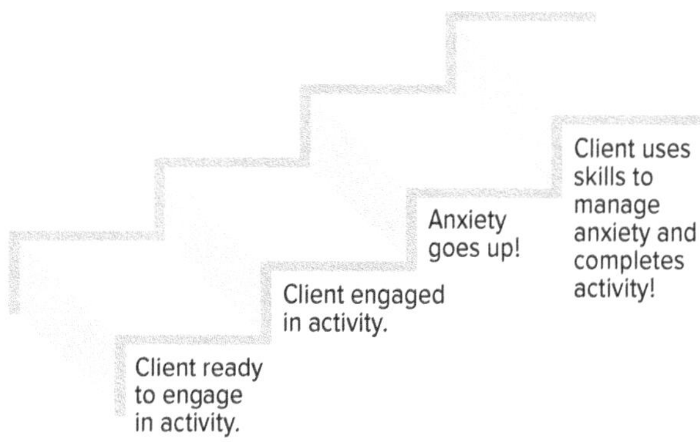

Figure 56

Target skill: Tolerating increased exposure to anxiety-provoking behaviors. Insight.

1. Begin with breathing. Ask your client to take three calm breaths with you. Take it slow. When you are done, explore with your client how comfortable she has become with using breath to calm herself. Ask: Is this becoming second nature? Does she practice calm breathing every day? If she does not, encourage her to do so at the beginning and end of every day.

2. Identify today's task: stepping up exposure. Congratulate your client on making it through the first intervention in spite of her anxiety. Say: *Now that you know it is possible to be anxious about something and do it anyway, we can move on to another difficult behavior.*

3. Review last week's homework: Inquire about your client engaging in the anxiety-provoking behavior. How difficult was this? You can use the scaling arrow to help your client gauge her level of anxiety before and during the activity. You should also ask what her level of anxiety was after the activity.

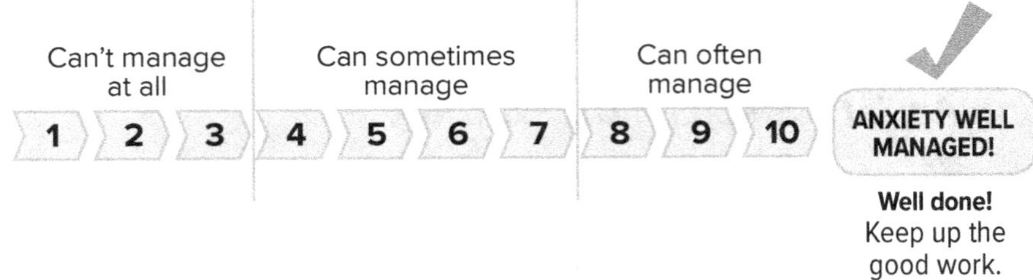

Figure 57

4. Work on today's task: Begin by explaining that if mild anxiety can be managed by using coping skills, then more anxiety can be managed, too. You can use the following image to help your client understand how exposure works.

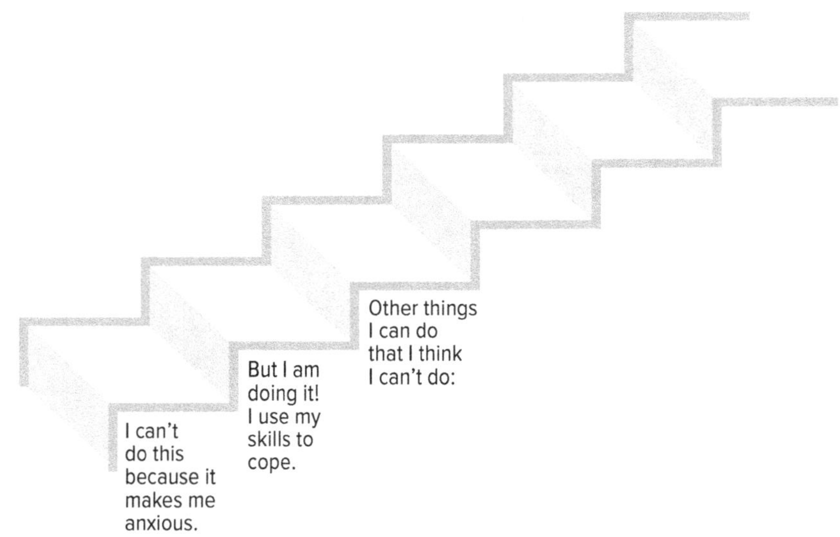

Figure 58

Help your client wonder out loud, like this:

> *If I can do* [the mildly anxiety provoking behavior your client has already engaged in], *then I can probably do* [the moderately anxiety provoking behavior you client will try to engage in].

Be sure to explain to your client that the next step should be one step up. It is best not to go three steps up because you want your client to be successful, and this means that she can manage her anxiety.

5. Ask your client to clearly identify the next step. This should be an activity or behavior that evokes moderate anxiety; on a scale from 1-3, this would be a 2. Ask your client to write that step on the stairs.

6. Help your client explore how she feels about taking the step. It is likely that your client becomes anxious. Help her manage the anxiety and talk about the proposed next step anyhow. You are engaging in exposure by thinking about the behavior. This is a great opportunity to practice skills.

7. Now plan ahead using the following chart:

Anxiety Provoking Behavior		
When I will engage in this behavior:	Day:	Time
What I will do if my anxiety level goes up:		
1.		
2.		
3.		
4.		

Figure 59

Add as many coping skills as you can. Because this behavior is predicted to cause moderate anxiety, you may need more or different coping skills. Help your client be fully prepared by asking:

What if your anxiety increases and you are beginning to feel overwhelmed?

8. Reinforce the idea that the activity must be completed. Avoidance cannot be an option, as this would reinforce the faulty idea that anxiety can't be managed!

9. Summarize today's work: You have taken one step up on the stairs of anxiety-provoking behaviors. You have first talked about the behavior (introspective exposure). You have then identified a number of coping skills your client can use when engaging in the activity in real life (*in vivo*). Your client has completed a coping chart to carry with her, as it is easy to forget things when under stress.

10. Assign homework: Send the chart home with your client. Ask your client to complete the identified behavior/activity using the coping skills identified.

11. Closing: Address any reluctance before your client leaves. Reinforce that anxiety is unsettling but will pass. You can use the metaphor of anxiety as a con man: Anxiety cons you to believe that you have to avoid certain behaviors, but this is just not true!

INTERVENTION 24

Facing Anxiety: Stepping to the Top

The following intervention is, in essence, a repetition. You will help your client (a) identify a behavior that is very anxiety provoking, (b) explore feelings and thoughts related to it, (c) prepare to engage in the behavior by identifying additional coping skills, and (d) engage in it in the real world.

You should only proceed to the "top" if your client was able to manage her anxiety and engage in the behavior causing her to have moderate anxiety.

The rating scale from 1 (provokes some anxiety) to 3 (provokes a lot of anxiety) is a suggestion. You can stretch this scale if needed. You client may need a scale from 1-5. This is OK.

Target skill: Tolerating exposure to high levels of anxiety-provoking behaviors. Insight about the nature of anxiety and ability to manage it.

1. Begin with breathing. Ask your client to take three calm breaths with you. Take it slow.

   When you are done, explore with your client how comfortable she has become with using breath to calm herself. Is this becoming second nature? Does she practice calm breathing every day? If she does not, encourage her to do so at the beginning and end of every day.

2. Identify today's task: making it to the top of the stairs. Explain that this may seem like a tall order, but that it really is not. Your client already knows how to use coping skills for anxiety! Taking one more step up can be scary, but it is really no different than the other steps.

3. Review last week's homework: Ask your client to discuss the moderately anxiety-provoking behavior with you. Did she engage in the behavior in spite of her anxiety? Which one of her coping skills worked best? (Make a note of that one, as you should use that one for today's intervention.) Which one did not help her? Was there a point at which she almost gave up? What kept her going?

   If your client did not complete the activity, find out why. Did her faulty thoughts get to her? Normalize failure as part of learning. Find out what went wrong, identify additional coping skills, and repeat the intervention.

4. Work on today's task: Making it to the top of the stairs.

   Begin by asking your client what behaviors and activities are most anxiety provoking. Try to get a feeling for the flavor of your client's anxiety. Is it mostly related to social interactions? Or perhaps feelings of inadequacy? Or fear of rejection? Help your client understand the themes of her anxieties.

   While you explore the themes and flavors of her most anxiety-provoking behaviors, you are once again engaging in introspective exposure. Help your client monitor her anxiety level using the scaling arrow. If necessary, move into using coping skills for anxiety. Generally speaking, once anxiety moves past 7 (on a 1–10 scale), it is a good idea to use coping skills to dial it down.

Keep in mind that coping skills are not a means to avoidance. Once anxiety is down again, resume talking about the anxiety-provoking behavior. Once you have explored and managed anxiety while talking about the behavior (introspective exposure), move into planning to engage in the behavior in real life. You can use the following chart to plan:

Anxiety Provoking Behavior		
When I will engage in this behavior:	Day:	Time
What I will do if my anxiety level goes up:		
1.		
2.		
3.		
4.		

Figure 60

Be sure to only list tried and true coping skills on the chart. If a coping skill did not work well for a moderately anxiety-provoking behavior, do not include it on this chart.

5. Summarize what you have done so far. You have identified a very anxiety-provoking behavior or activity and explored it (introspective exposure). You have then made a plan to engage in the behavior and have identified coping skills that fit the situation.

6. Now is a good time to remind your client that anxiety is just the body's response to a real or perceived threat. More often than not, anxiety, the great con man, is tricking her into believing that she can't do something she can actually do.

7. Assign homework: Send your client home with the chart and ask her to engage in the anxiety-provoking activity. Remind her that she has the skills to succeed.

8. Closing: Be sure to ask about any barriers that might stand in the way of homework completion. Here are some typical barriers:

   - Your client is just saying "yes" but is still really scared to complete the homework.
   - Your client forgets about homework.
   - Your client does not believe that exposure can work for her.

Address any questions or concerns your client may have to make sure she will complete the homework.

INTERVENTION 25

Working with Failure

This intervention addresses the need to work with "failure." You can address perceived failure by reframing it as part of the learning process. You can also find success within failure. If your client completed part of the exposure exercises, then she was partly successful.

Target skill: Overcoming perfectionism in symptom management. Acceptance. Insight.

1. Begin with breathing. Ask your client to take three calm breaths with you. Take it slow. When you are done, explore with your client how comfortable she has become with using breath to calm herself. Is this becoming second nature? Does she practice calm breathing every day? If she does not, encourage her to do so at the beginning and end of every day.

2. Check in with your client: How does she feel about exposing herself to anxiety-provoking thoughts and behaviors? Is she beginning to gain a sense that anxiety is manageable? That she can walk through the storm of anxiety and find calm on the other side?

3. Identify today's task: Working with "failure."

   - Help your client identify situations in which she thought she failed. Perhaps she did not fully complete an assignment or was too scared to tell you she did not succeed.

   - Listen to your client with compassion.

   - Identify thinking errors, such as, "I failed, therefore I am a failure," or "I failed, and my therapist thinks I am a failure/my therapist hates me."

   - Explain that you will work on integrating perceived failure into treatment.

   - Explain that failure is to be expected. It is a normal part of life. So is success.

4. Review last week's homework: Ask about your client's experience of engaging in the very anxiety-provoking activity. Listen carefully as your client tells the story. Is she telling you what happened with pride? Is the experience of talking to you about this anxiety provoking? Pay attention to your client's body language and facial expressions. If needed, help her through the experience by using your breath and posture to help her regulate.

   If your client perceived that she has failed in some way, explore this with her and reframe perceived failure as an opportunity to learn more about her anxiety and how to manage it. If your client avoided the activity, explore the idea of anxiety having a friend: the big bad bully of avoidance. The big bad bully of avoidance tells you that everything will be better if you just don't engage in anything that provokes anxiety. The trouble with this, of course, is that the bully is lying.

5. Work on today's task: working with failure using the following worksheet:

Things I can say to the failure/avoidance bully:
You are a liar!
. . .

Things I can do about the failure/avoidance bully:
Anticipate that he will show up.
Be prepared for his lies.
. . .

How I can welcome the failure/avoidance bully without believing his message:
Listen, but not believe his words . . .
. . .

Figure 62

What you are trying to do, once again, is help your client understand that the avoidance bully has no power. She does not have to listen to him (you are now working within the cognitive element of the triad). Or she could listen with compassion. If your client suggests that she could just run away from the failure bully, say this:

Bullies usually chase you. How about facing instead of running?

Here are ways of listening to the failure bully with compassion:

- Ask the bully what made him so very pessimistic. What has happened to him?
- Teach the avoidance bully calm breathing to help him calm down.
- Ask the avoidance bully if he is lonely.
- Ask the avoidance bully if he needs a friend.

6. Help your client complete the worksheet using Socratic questions. Suggest that it is possible to embrace perceived failure as part of the process of learning to manage anxious thoughts, feelings, and behaviors. Ask:

    - *How can you embrace failure as a part of the process of managing anxiety?*
    - *In what way can failure be helpful?*
    - *How can you be kind to failure?*
    - *How can you be kind to yourself when you perceive that you have failed?*

7. Summarize what you have done together today:

    - You have explored the many ways in which failure can be like a bully.
    - You identified how your client can face the bully of avoidance and failure and embrace perceived failure as part of the process of learning to manage anxiety.

8. Identify new homework: Send your client home with the avoidance bully worksheet. Ask her to use the different ways she has identified to talk back to the bully. If a specific response worked, she should use a highlighter to mark it. Ask her to bring the worksheet back to your next meeting.

9. Closing: Before your client leaves, acknowledge how powerful bully messages can be. But this does not mean that they are true. You can say this: *If you know that a dish is poisoned, you will not eat it. Bully messages are poison. Don't take them in!*

INTERVENTION 26

When Anxiety Returns

Talk with your client about the sometimes cyclical nature of anxiety. Your client may feel that once she has made it to the top of the stairs and engaged in her most anxiety-provoking activity that her anxiety about this should be gone. This intervention helps your client understand that anxiety can come in waves. It can and often does return. This should not be viewed as an indicator of personal failure, but rather as the nature of things. Anxiety can be cyclical. When it returns, it is just time to once again step up the stairs.

Target skill: Understanding cyclical nature of anxiety. Coping with returning anxiety.

1. Begin with breathing. Ask your client to take three calm breaths with you. Take it slow. When you are done, explore with your client how comfortable she has become with using breathing to calm herself. Ask: Is this becoming second nature? Does she practice calm breathing every day? If she does not, encourage her to do so at the beginning and end of every day.

2. Identify today's task: managing the waves of anxiety as they come and go. You can show your client the following image to illustrate:

Figure 63

   Introduce the idea that some days the seas are calm and some days there a lot of waves. This is just the nature of things. It does not mean your client has done anything wrong or has failed.

3. Review last week's homework: Ask your client if she used the bully worksheet when her anxiety tried to push her into avoidance. Which ideas, thoughts, or behaviors from the bully worksheet worked well? Explore the ones she highlighted. Those will now become your client's go-to defenses against the bully of avoidance.

4. Work on today's task:

   - Begin by asking your client about her experience of anxiety about behaviors. How persistent is it? You will get a sense of how deeply rooted her anxiety is.

   - Return to the image of the ocean. Sometimes the waves are calm:

Figure 64

- Ask your client to explore a calm, relatively anxiety-free day in her life, a day when she successfully engaged in a normally anxiety-provoking behavior without much trouble.

- Next, ask your client to explore a day that was more difficult. Perhaps she wanted to avoid anxiety-provoking behaviors. It might be the kind of day where it seems there is a shark lurking in the water.

Figure 65

- Help your client explore the idea that the weather changes and sometimes there will be waves. Ask your client what she should do when a wave of anxiety about behaviors is approaching again. This is a good way to ascertain that your client understands she just needs to go back to using her coping skills. If necessary, review your client's most effective coping skills with her. Remind her that she has successfully managed her anxiety in the past and can do so again.

- You may want to introduce the idea of "riding the wave" instead of fighting it. You can't fight the ocean, but you can bring a surfboard. Your coping skills are your surfboard.

- What if your client is frustrated? She just wants to get rid of all of her anxiety.

- Work with your client on realistic thinking. Anxiety is based on fear. Fear has a function (to keep you alive). Help your client explore situations in which fear was useful. Help her understand that anxiety is just fear gone too far. It can be reigned-in. Fear is a part of life and, to a certain degree, so is anxiety. The ocean will have waves when there are storms. But there are also times of calm with few waves.

5. Summarize what you have done so far: Together you have examined the cyclical nature of anxiety about behaviors. You have thought about stormy seas, when the waves of anxiety are high, and calm seas, when anxiety is low and almost anything seems possible. You have used the metaphor of riding the waves of anxiety using a surfboard.

6. Assign homework: Ask your client to use the following chart to document the kinds of waves and weather she experiences over the next few days. Ask her to draw calm seas, little waves, gigantic waves, or anything in between to document the kinds of day she is having. Also ask her to write down any anxiety-provoking behaviors for that day. Notes can be written on the back. Ask your client to bring this chart to your next meeting.

Riding the waves: Draw the "waves" for every day
Monday:
Tuesday:
Wednesday:
Thursday:
Friday:
Saturday:
Sunday:

Figure 66

7. Closing: Check in with your client. Does she have any questions? If she struggles with the metaphor of the waves, she can either write things down or invent her own metaphor.

Exposure: Jumping for Joy

So far you have exposed your client to anxious thoughts about behaviors, actions, and events. Engaging in exposure can be exhausting. When it seems that your client is having a hard time with engaging in another exposure intervention, try sprinkling in a joy exposure.

Target skill: Using joy to cope with exposure to anxiety-provoking behaviors.

1. Begin with breathing. Ask your client to take three calm breaths with you. Take it slow. When you are done, explore with your client how comfortable she has become with using breath to calm herself. Ask: Is this becoming second nature? Does she practice calm breathing every day? If she does not, encourage her to do so at the beginning and end of every day.

2. Identify today's task: experiencing joy in spite of all the difficult and anxious experiences your client may have every day. Say: *There has to be room for joy— and we are going to find it.*

3. Review last week's homework: Look at the chart your client brought. What kinds of waves did she draw? Ask about each day. Instead of focusing how difficult the week might have been and how many high waves there were, focus on the things your client has done well in spite of the waves. Ask: *When and how did you ride the waves? What kind of ride was it?*

4. Work on today's task: Begin by asking your client what gives her pure joy. What is pure joy? Pure joy is the kind of joy that just happens. It is a full-body experience. Here are some examples of how pure joy can happen:

   - dancing wildly to favorite music

   - jumping for joy

   - holding a calm baby

   - sled-riding

   - laughing with a friend

Figure 67

5. Ask your client what brings her pure joy. Ask her to describe in detail what pure joy feels like. Then help her explore how her mind and body feel when she talks about pure joy. You may want to comment on your client's smile, animated body language, or laughter.

6. Now: Ask your client to identify one appropriate thing that gives her pure joy that can be done or can happen almost anywhere. Here are some examples:
   - jumping for joy
   - somersaulting
   - dancing wildly (if only for a moment)
   - thinking of an outing with your best friend
   - singing along to loud music
   - blowing bubbles

7. If at all possible (and appropriate), engage in the joy activity together. You can get music on your phone. Somersaulting may be tricky in the office (but not impossible). Of course, your client should only pick activities she can actually engage in. If she struggles moving, it's quite possible to dance in a chair.

8. Help your client reflect on the experience of joy. Say: *While it is important to practice exposure to anxiety-provoking behaviors, it is equally important to get joy exposure. It balances things out.*

9. Summarize what you have done today: You have explored the importance of experiencing joy, and you have experienced joy together.

10. Assign new homework: Give your client the joy card.

Figure 68

Ask her to write her joy activity on the card and take the card home. Ask your client to carry the card with her and engage in her joy activity at least once every day.

11. Closing: Before your client leaves, say: ***Joy is important. It can fill our whole mind and our whole body. It is also free. It is important to make joy a part of our lives every day.***

Expanding the Window of Tolerance

Every one of us has a range and intensity of emotions we can tolerate. There are several components to using exposure:

- We want our clients to learn that anxiety responses to certain behaviors can be eliminated. Once we engage in an anxiety-provoking behavior, we "disarm" anxiety. It may still be there, but it no longer keeps us from living our lives.

- Additionally, we are asking our clients to expand their window of tolerance. Anxiety feels dangerous. Therein lies its power. If your client can learn, bit by bit, to tolerate more and more anxiety, she becomes able to engage in behaviors even if the anxiety is still present.

Target skill: Expanding range of tolerable emotions and behaviors.

1. Begin with breathing. Ask your client to take three calm breaths with you. Take it slow. When you are done, explore with your client how comfortable she has become with using breath to calm herself. Ask: Is this becoming second nature? Does she practice calm breathing every day? If she does not, encourage her to do so at the beginning and end of every day.

2. Identify today's task: expanding the Window of Tolerance of Anxiety that occurs in response to engaging in anxiety-provoking behaviors. You can explain the idea of a window of tolerance using this image:

Figure 69

This is a small window of tolerance. Because I am anxious, I only see a very small part of the world. There may be other things out there, but I don't see them.

The task today will be to make the window larger.

3. Review last week's homework: Ask to see your client's Joy Card. If she has it with her, this is a good indicator that she may be using it. If she does not have it with her, ask her if she knows where it is. You could also give her a new one and reiterate the importance of following through with her homework. Explain that treatment progress is connected with practice.

    If your client did use her Joy Card, ask her how it worked. What kind of a difference does it make to purposefully practice joy? What were her joy experiences like? Can she imagine sharing pure joy with someone?

4. Work on today's task: Show your client the small window again. Ask her:

    - *What do you think is out there that you are not seeing because the window is so small?*

    - *What are the things out there that you would like to see but can't because the window is so small?* Ask your client to be specific about this.

    - *What would it be like to have a larger window?* How much does your client want to see? What does she not want to see?

5. Give your client this image of a larger window of tolerance:

Figure 70

Ask your client to draw and write in all the things she would be able to see if the window was larger. She should include things she really wants to see (perhaps trees) and things she does not really want to see, but would see, because they are there (such as chimneys from a factory).

6. Help your client explore and understand that in order to have a full vision and experience of all that is in the world, she will see and experience pleasant and unpleasant things. You can't have one without the other.

   Say: ***Anxiety makes your window to the world very small and gives you the illusion that you can avoid anxiety-inducing behaviors and experiences. But they are still out there.***

7. Suggest the strategy of expanding the window of tolerance. Here is how it might work.

   Start with a small window of tolerance:

Figure 71

   This is your baseline. Your client is very anxious and avoids behaviors that are anxiety provoking. List three important behaviors your client avoids.

8. Expand the window a little bit:

Figure 72

What can your client now see that she did not see before?

9. Ask your client which behavior she currently avoids that would give her a larger window to the world. What would she have to do to expand her window? What would she gain if she did?

You may want to use the following chart to help your client understand why expanding the window of tolerance is a good idea:

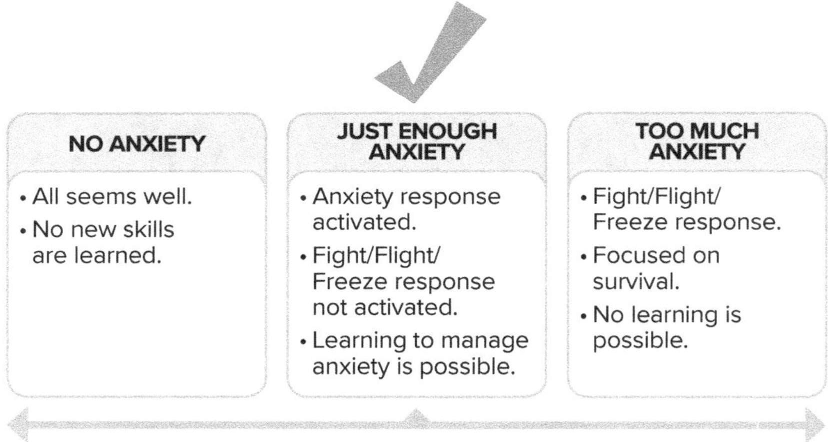

Figure 73

10. The Million-Dollar Question: How do you expand the window of tolerance? For most of our clients the answer is: bit by bit. Help your client move from a very small window of tolerance to a small one to a medium one and so forth. If this is helpful, work with the image of a window getting larger bit by bit.

11. Be sure to help your client reflect on each step. How does it feel to have a larger window of tolerance?

12. Summarize what you have done today: You have introduced the metaphor of a window of tolerance and have explored what it would be like to have a larger window.

13. Assign new homework: Identify one way your client can expand her window of tolerance this week. Write it on an index card and be sure to help your client identify coping skills that will help her manage her anxiety on the card, too. Send the card home with your client and ask her to do the one thing she named to expand her window of tolerance:

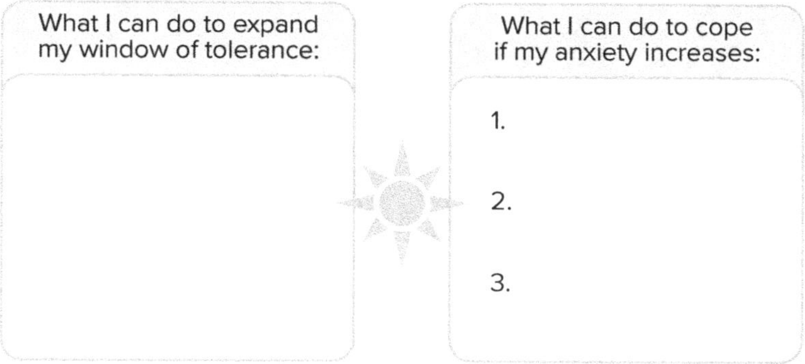

Figure 74

14. Closing: Send your client home with thoughts of hope. Say: *You can expand your window of tolerance bit by bit. Anxiety may be a part of the process, but you can cope with it.* If your client feels reluctant to give the assignment a try, encourage her to listen to both her reluctance (it will help her plan for appropriate coping skills) and her courage (she wants to experience more of the world and become a more active participant in life).

Walking Out the Door

This intervention builds on the metaphor of the window of tolerance. Once your client has experienced that it is possible to expand the window of tolerance bit by bit, she may be ready to simply stop looking out of windows and walk out the door, living her life fully.

Does this mean her anxiety will be gone? For many people it does not. But their anxiety has decreased, and they are also better able to tolerate it.

Target skill: Anxiety-coping by moving focus away from anxious behaviors and thoughts.

1. Begin with breathing. Ask your client to take three calm breaths with you. Take it slow. When you are done, explore with your client how comfortable she has become with using breath to calm herself. Ask: Is this becoming second nature? Does she practice calm breathing every day? If she does not, encourage her to do so at the beginning and end of every day.

2. Identify today's task: walking out the door instead of looking out of the window. You can explain this metaphor using the following story:

   There once was a woman who worked very hard to overcome her anxiety. She went to therapy every week, and every week she learned to listen to her curiosity more and listen to her anxiety less. She was now doing things she never thought she could do. She went to the pool and wore a bathing suit in public. She went on a date. She started working at a job. And she went to see her mother (now that one was hard).

   She was still anxious when she did those things, but she did them anyway. She was very conscious about expanding her window of tolerance.

   One day she decided that she was done with looking out of windows of whatever size. She would no longer need to make windows larger and larger.

   She would simply do the things she needed and wanted to do. And that's what she did. Sometimes she was anxious about things. And she did them anyway. Sometimes she was not anxious. She just lived her life.

3. Review last week's homework: How was your client able to expand her window of tolerance? What went well? Which coping skill worked? Be sure to celebrate the small steps. If the window of tolerance expanded just an inch, this is progress. Progress does not have to include a perfectly executed assignment.

4. Work on today's task: Ask your client to envision a life in which she no longer is defined by her anxiety about behaviors, but simply lives her life. In

other words, she no longer needs to expand her window of opportunity. Ask your client to tell the story above, but in her own manner about her own life.

5. If your client feels that she is not quite there, ask her to try to tell the story anyway. Validate that although it can be difficult to walk out the door, it is quite possible. If your client struggles with inventing her own story, use the above story and ask her to fill in the blanks:

> There once was a woman who worked very hard to overcome her anxiety. She went to therapy every week and every week she learned to listen to her curiosity more and listen to her anxiety less. She was now doing things she never thought she could do. She _____________and_______________. She___________. She started_______________. And she _______________ (now that one was hard).
>
> She was still anxious when she did those things, but she did them anyway. She was very conscious about expanding her window of tolerance.
>
> One day she decided that she was done with______________________________. She would no longer need to_______________________.
>
> She would simply do the things she needed to and wanted to do. And that's what she did. Sometimes she was anxious about things. And she did them anyway. Sometimes she was not anxious. She just lived her life.

6. Once your client has finished telling her story, help her reflect on how this felt. Does it feel liberating to think about living her life? Or does it feel scary? If it feels scary, what does this mean?

7. Show your client the arrow of therapeutic progress:

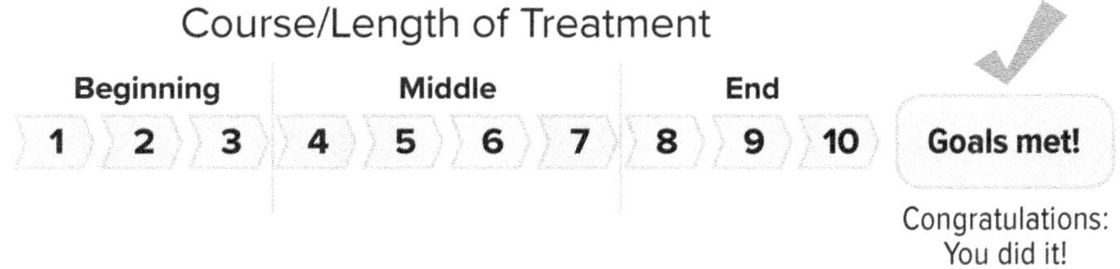

Figure 75

Where does she view herself in the process of treatment? Help your client clearly identify the progress she has made and begin discussing that possibility of termination.

8. If your client becomes anxious about the prospect of termination, this is to be expected. Acknowledge this with her and help her habituate, bit by bit, to the thought of termination.

9. Summarize what you have done today: You have thought about the possibility of being done with therapy. You have done so by listening to a story and by telling a story. You have also used the arrow of therapeutic progress to help gauge your client's progress and begin to help her habituate to the (possibly anxiety provoking) thought of termination of services.

10. Assign new homework: Give your client an index card with the arrow of therapeutic progress. Ask her to write on the back of the card what still needs to happen for her to consider treatment complete and bring the card to your next meeting.

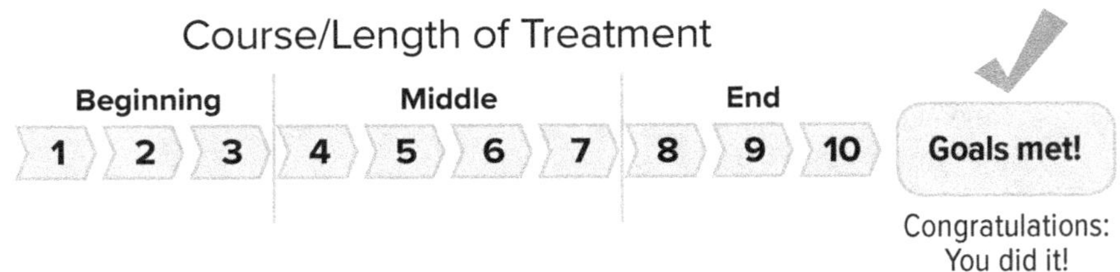

Figure 76

11. Closing: Send your client home with words of encouragement: *Yes, it is possible to be done with treatment. And you are getting closer. It is OK if this feels scary. You can overcome your anxiety about ending treatment.*

INTERVENTION 30

Ending Treatment

Your client has come a long way. She is now able to engage in behaviors she never thought she could. Things are not perfect. Perhaps she is still somewhat anxious about a few things. But she knows her coping skills and she uses them. It is time to end treatment.

Target skill: Insight about anxiety coping.

1. Begin with breathing. Ask your client to take three calm breaths with you. Take it slow. When you are done, explore with your client how comfortable she has become with using breath to calm herself. Ask: Is this becoming second nature? Does she practice calm breathing every day?

2. Identify today's task: ending treatment. You may want to ask your client to take another deep breath together at this point to recognize the significance of the event. Acknowledge that it is OK to have feelings about this.

3. Review last week's homework: Ask your client to show you the index card with the arrow of therapeutic progress. Check in with your client. Where does she view herself?

    - Then examine together if her view of her treatment progress is realistic. Use the evidence of what you have done together to correctly identify where your client is in treatment. If there are still a few things to do before treatment can end, then plan together on doing them.

    - If your client feels that treatment can never end because she will never be ready to face her anxiety (or get rid of all of it), plan for a session of cognitive work on thinking errors about what constitutes progress and what your client has learned or not learned.

    - If you disagree about treatment progress, use evidence from therapy sessions to support your position and ask your client to do the same. This is another opportunity to practice realistic thinking instead of overly positive or pessimistic thinking.

4. Work on today's task: Getting your client ready for termination.

    - Ask your client to remember beginning treatment. What were all the things she did not do because of her anxiety? What did it feel like to come to therapy?

    - Then ask your client to acknowledge all the things she is doing now, perhaps in spite of her anxiety or even without feeling anxious.

    - Help your client acknowledge all the progress she has made. Emphasize that she did the hard work.

    - Acknowledge that change can be anxiety provoking, but this does not mean she needs to stay in treatment forever.

- Help your client create a memento of the work you have done together. For some clients this can mean creating a certificate of completion or success. There are many free templates available on the Internet. Other clients may select a soothing image or a small object to remind them of the work you did together. What your client chooses is dependent on personality and age. It should be appropriate and not costly.

5. Summarize the work you did today: You worked on recognizing the progress your client has made. You have created a memento your client can take with her to remind her of the work you did together.

6. No homework today!

7. Closing: Remind your client that the work of managing anxiety continues and that it is important to keep up the good work of using coping skills such as calm breathing. Wish your client well. She now has what she needs to do what she wants to do.

Interventions Working with the Emotional Component of the Triad

By now it should be clear that the components of the triad we are working in are interconnected. This means that if you are working with your client on negative thoughts, you are also secondarily working on negative behaviors and emotions. Feelings can be an easy door for many of our clients to walk through to begin to make changes. Our clients often come to us often with raw, unprocessed feelings, and many just want them to go away. The following interventions are designed to help your client move from those raw and unprocessed feelings into thoughtful evaluation.

INTERVENTION 31

The Flood

This intervention will help your client explore and understand the nature of her anxious feelings, the way they rush in and seem unstoppable. She will learn that anxious feelings, like anxious thoughts, can be examined when taking a step back.

Target skill: Insight about anxious feelings.

1. Begin with breathing. Ask your client to take three calm breaths with you. Take it slow. When you are done, explore with your client how comfortable this is. In what way is her body now functioning differently?

2. Welcome your client and check in. How is your client managing her anxious feelings? Ask your client to describe what happens when she feels anxious.

3. Identify today's task: examining how your client views anxious feelings and how they may be contained. You can explain this task by telling the following story:

   > *There once was a river. It flowed through the meadow, and it was no trouble at all. When there was rain, it would rise a little bit, but then the water would go down again. But one day things changed. It just kept raining and raining for days. And the river kept rising. It finally flooded. It flooded the streets. It flooded the basements. It even flooded the town's school. And now things were on hold. There was no school. And no traffic.*
   >
   > *When the rains stopped, the townspeople began cleaning up. It took them quite a while. And when they were all done, they called a meeting and decided to make a plan. They did not want to get caught in a flood again. There were going to make sure of this.*

4. Work on today's task. Ask your client:

   - *In what way is your anxiety like a flood?*

   - *In what way are you bothered by it?*

   - *In what way does it surprise you?*

   - *How predictable is it?*

   - *What do you think the townspeople should do? How should they prepare for the next flood?*

   - *What do you think would not work for the townspeople?*

5. Now ask your client to explore with you what she does when she feels anxious. Does she get swept away by the flood of her anxious feelings? Does she feel like she is going under?

6. Help your client understand that there are a couple of ways of dealing with the flood of anxious feelings. Here is an image that might help:

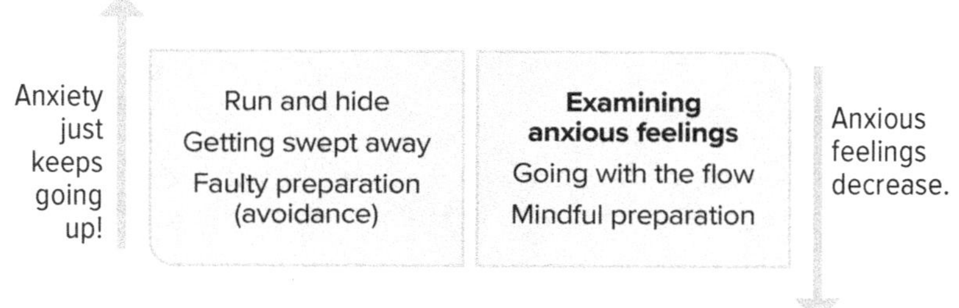

Figure 77

7. Ask your client to explore how she tries to run and hide from her anxious feelings and in what way she prepares for them. Ask:

    - *What would mindful preparation look like?*

    - *What would happen if you just let the anxious feelings happen and observed them?*

8. Ask your client to go back in her mind to the idea of anxious feelings being like a flood. What would happen if she could step back and observe the flood of her feelings from a safe distance? How would she describe the flood?

9. Ask: *What kind of flotation device or boat would you need if you had to go with the flow of the flood? Do you think this is even possible?*

10. Summarize what you have done so far.

    - You have used the image of anxiety as a flood to help your client examine what happens when she feels anxious.

    - You have introduced the idea that there are different ways of relating to those anxious feelings. By doing so you have begun to help your client understand that anxious feelings, like most things, can be examined.

11. Assign homework: Ask your client to explore the following ideas about the flood of anxious feelings:

    - *What is it like to get swept away by anxious feelings?*

    - *What would it be like to go with the flow of anxious feelings instead?*

    Give your client an index card to write down notes about these questions and ask her to bring the cards back to your next meeting.

12. Closing: As your client prepares to go home, ask her to step back from her flood of anxious feelings and observe them instead of getting caught up in them.

INTERVENTION 32

Going with the Flow

This intervention continues to work with the metaphor of anxiety as a flood. In this case you will help your client invent different ways of letting anxiety happen without getting swept away by it.

Target skill: Working with and coping with anxious feelings.

1. Begin with breathing. Ask your client to take three calm breaths with you. Take it slow. When you are done, explore with your client how comfortable she is. In what way is her body now functioning differently?

2. Welcome your client. Ask how the last week went. What went well? What did not go well? Help your client gauge the intensity of her anxious feelings using the scaling arrow.

Figure 78

3. Identify today's task: learning to go with the flow. Explain that anxious feelings seem dangerous. This can activate our fight/flight response. Explain that today you will try to figure out together how to not activate the fight/flight response, but rather learn to go with the flow of anxious feelings, letting them happen, without letting them do harm.

4. Review last week's homework: Ask your client to take out her index card from last week and explore with her what it feels like to be swept away by anxious feelings. Ask: *If something could be done about this, would you want to do it?*

5. Work on today's task: going with the flow instead of fighting the flood. Ask:

    - *If you could go with the flow, what kind of flotation device or boat would you need?*

    - *How big would you want your boat to be?*

    - *What material?*

    - *Is there equipment on board? What kind?*

    - *Who would you like with you?*

Help your client explore these questions in detail, as the answers may give you a sense of her anxious feelings.

Will your client be in a yacht or on a surfboard?

6. Now ask your client to think of herself as a master surfer. You can tell her the following story to help her imagine this:

> *There once was a master surfer. She had ridden so many waves that she had become one with the water. She could sense every wave even before it came. When it came, her body and mind were fully prepared. She would simply listen to her body and mind and ride the waves. Even the big ones. Even in a storm. She went with the flow of waves with ease because she understood them to be a part of things that she was also a part of.*

Ask your client:

- *How can you ride the waves of anxious feelings?*

- *How would you have to think about anxious feelings in order to stop fearing them?*

- *What would it feel like to be on top of and ride the waves of anxiety instead of fighting the current?*

- *Where do you think the waves would take you?*

7. Summarize what you have done so far:

- You have explored the idea of going with the flow and riding the waves of feelings of anxiety as opposed to fighting them.

- You have explored together what kind of flotation device or boat your client would want to ride the waves, and you have introduced the idea of becoming a master surfer of the waves of anxious feelings.

In essence, you have explored how your client can have a different relationship with her anxious feelings. They only have the power that we give them. If you change how you relate to those feelings, you change the power they have over you!

8. Identify new homework. Give your client the following story on an index card to take home and read every day/once per day:

> *I am a master surfer. I have ridden so many waves that I have become one with the water. I can sense every wave even before it comes. When it comes, my body and mind are fully prepared. I simply listen to my body and mind and ride the waves. Even the big ones. Even in a storm. I go with the flow of waves with ease, because I understand them to be a part of things that I am also a part of.*

9. Closing: As you send your client home, ask her to think of herself as a surfer of the waves of anxious feelings. Say: *You can be on top of this!*

INTERVENTION 33

Being Well Prepared for the Flood of Anxious Thoughts Versus Frantic Preparation

So perhaps your client is able to think about surfing the waves of her anxious thoughts with ease, but she can't quite do so yet. This intervention is designed to help your client prepare for the flood in an effective as opposed to a frantic way.

Target skill: Planning ahead to cope with anxious feelings. Acceptance. Insight.

1. Begin with breathing. Ask your client to take three calm breaths with you. Take it slow. When you are done, explore with your client how comfortable she is. In what way is her body now functioning differently?

2. Welcome your client. Ask how the last week went. What went well? What did not go well? Help your client gauge the intensity of her anxious feelings using the scaling arrow.

Figure 79

3. Identify today's task: mindful preparation for anxious feelings. You can explain that preparing for anxious feelings can take away some of their power. Being prepared also acknowledges the reality of anxiety in your client's life: She does not have to run from anxiety.

4. Review last week's homework: Ask your client to take out the master surfer index card (always have a backup copy ready) and read it to you. Then inquire: Did you carry your card with you? What did it feel like to read it daily? In what way are you a master surfer? In what way are you not a master surfer yet?

   Then switch. Read the card to your client substituting "I" with "you." Ask: *What is different if I read this to you?*

5. Work on today's task. Take another look at the basic ways of dealing with anxious feelings chart:

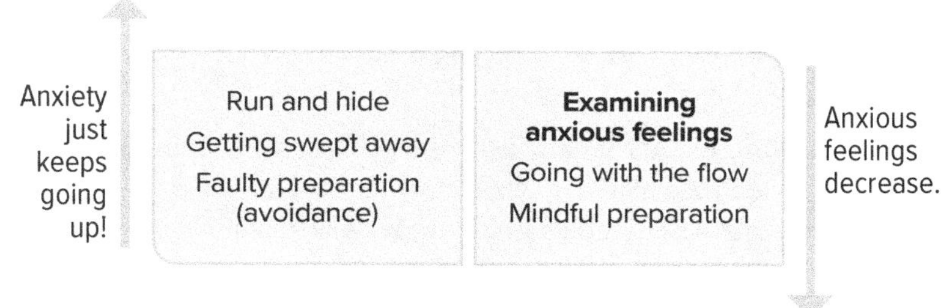

Figure 80

Explain that today you are going to work on mindful preparation for anxious feelings. Ask: ***What do you need to be prepared for anxious feelings?***

6. Help your client create a list of effective ways to prepare. The important thing is to accept that anxious feelings are going to happen, so thoughtful preparation is a good thing. Here are some things that are not thoughtful preparation:

   - making a plan to avoid anxious feelings at all times through distraction

   - other forms of running away from anxious feelings

   - being angry about anxious feelings

   - blaming others for the presence or content of anxious feelings

   - fear-based preparation, like, "This is going to be terrible."

   Here are some ways to mindfully prepare:

   - practicing calm breathing

   - reading the master surfer card

   - listening to calming music

   - telling a friend about the anxious feelings while staying calm

   - observing the anxious feelings from afar with kindness

7. Here is a preparation chart you can complete with your client:

Mindful preparation for anxious feelings
Breathe:
Sing:
Talk to a friend:

Figure 81

Be sure to be specific about preparation. What breathing exercise is your client going to use? Who is she going to talk to? What song is she going to sing?

8. Explain to your client that any time is a good time for mindful preparation for anxious feelings. Waiting until those feelings arrive is not a good idea. If mindful preparation is a part of her daily life, then she will be prepared no matter when the anxious feeling arrives!

9. Summarize what you have done today: You have identified faulty ways to prepare for anxious feelings (mainly avoidance and frantic action) and mindful ways to prepare.

10. Assign homework: Give your client her mindful preparation chart and ask her to practice each item on the list at least once over the course of the next week (there should be seven things on the list). Ask your client to check things off as she goes, and bring the chart back to your next session.

11. Closing: As you send your client home, ask her to view anxious feelings that may come up as opportunities to practice surfing the waves!

INTERVENTION 34

The Observer

This intervention takes yet another approach to facing the flood of anxious feelings. You will ask your client to become an observer of her anxious feelings. An observer can take a curious stance and examine what emotional responses are appropriate for the situation and what responses are not a good fit.

Target skill: Defusion from anxious feelings.

1. Begin with breathing. Ask your client to take three calm breaths with you. Take it slow. When you are done, explore with your client how comfortable she is. In what way is her body now functioning differently?

2. Welcome your client. Ask how the last week went. What went well? What did not go well? Help your client gauge the intensity of her anxious feelings using the scaling arrow.

3. Identify today's task: becoming an observer of anxious feelings. You can say this: *An observer can be a scientist. An observer can examine what works and what does not work.* Wonder out loud with your client: *What would it be like to observe a flood of anxious feelings as opposed to being swept away by them?*

4. Review last week's homework: Look at the mindful preparation chart. What worked preparing for anxious feelings? What did not work? Highlight what worked, and make those things the go-to preparation activities.

5. Work on today's task. Tell your client to imagine the following:

   You are sitting high above the riverbed at the top of a hill. You are close enough to see the flood waters rush by, but far away enough not to be scared. You watch the high waters rush by. Those are your anxious feelings. They are certainly powerful. They move fast.

   But you are not immersed in the water. You are observing the flood from a safe distance.

6. Take out a piece of paper and drawing tools and help your client create a simple image of what you have described. Remind your client that this exercise is not about her drawing skills, but rather about her ability to become an observer.

7. Look at the drawing your client has created. How high up is she? How far away from the flood? Examine the image together with your client.

8. Move into examining the metaphor of becoming an observer of the flood of anxious feelings. Here are some questions you may want to use:

   - *How can you put yourself in a position of distance to your feelings? This does not mean ignoring them; it just means you are not fully immersed in them.*

- *How do you feel about becoming an observer of your anxious feelings? Does this seem like a great idea? Or do you feel like you are "betraying" your feelings?*

- *How difficult is it for you to observe your own feelings?*

9. Ask your client to remember an anxious feeling perhaps from the day before. Write the feeling (situation, intensity, experience of it) on a piece of paper and then ask your client to look at it. You can say this: *You had this feeling yesterday. That creates some distance. How can you create this feeling of distance for intense anxious feelings you are experiencing in the moment?*

10. Summarize what you have done together today: You have used the metaphor of a flood or rushing river to help your client explore how she can become an observer of her anxious feelings. You have looked at the idea of being close to anxious feelings and gaining some distance from them.

11. Identify new homework: Give your client a set of seven index cards. Instruct her to write an anxious feeling on each index card as it happens and then place the card at a distance from her.

    She should say to herself: "There it is, my anxious feeling. It is over there. I am over here. From over here my anxious feeling looks different, less frightening. I can observe it and examine it." Ask your client to bring back the anxious feelings cards to your next meeting.

12. Closing: Check in with your client. Does she have any questions? Are there any barriers to completing the homework?

INTERVENTION 35

The Examiner

This intervention builds upon the prior one and asks your client to venture further into the role of examining anxious feelings like a scientist.

Target skill: Defusion from anxious feelings. Evaluation of anxious feelings. Insight.

1. Begin with breathing. Ask your client to take three calm breaths with you. Take it slow. When you are done, explore with your client how comfortable this is. In what way is her body now functioning differently?

2. Welcome your client. Ask how the last week went. What went well? What did not go well? Help your client gauge the intensity of her anxious feelings using the scaling arrow.

3. Identity today's task: closely examining anxious feelings. Here are some questions you will use:

   - *How does this feeling fit reality?*

   - *In what way does the intensity of the feeling fit reality? In what way does it not?*

   - *Does this feeling belong with the current situation?*

4. Homework Review: Ask your client to take out her anxious feelings cards. Look at the anxious feelings she has named. Ask her to pick one card and explore with you how she used the card and the associated saying.

   There it is, my anxious feeling. It is over there. I am over here. From over here my anxious feeling looks different, less frightening. I can observe it and examine it.

5. Work on today's task: Today you are moving into the heart of CBT. You are going to ask: *Is this feeling realistic? Does it fit with reality as it is right now?*

   What if your client does not want to devalue her feelings?

   Examining a feeling to see if it is realistic does not mean you are negating it. You are, however, examining the truth of the feeling. Just because we feel something does not mean the feeling relates to reality as it is right now. It could relate to something in the past.

6. Use the following chart to help your client examine an anxious feeling. It might be a good idea to use an anxious feeling that frequently bothers your client.

The Anxious Feeling:
What does this feeling tell me?
What is the evidence that the message the feeling sends me is true?
What is the evidence that the message the feeling sends me is not true?
Where does the feeling originate? Is it an old feeling?
How can I be present with what is happening right now?

Figure 82

7. Help your client understand that she is moving from simply believing the message of the anxious feeling to examining it and putting it in its rightful place. Here is an image that may help:

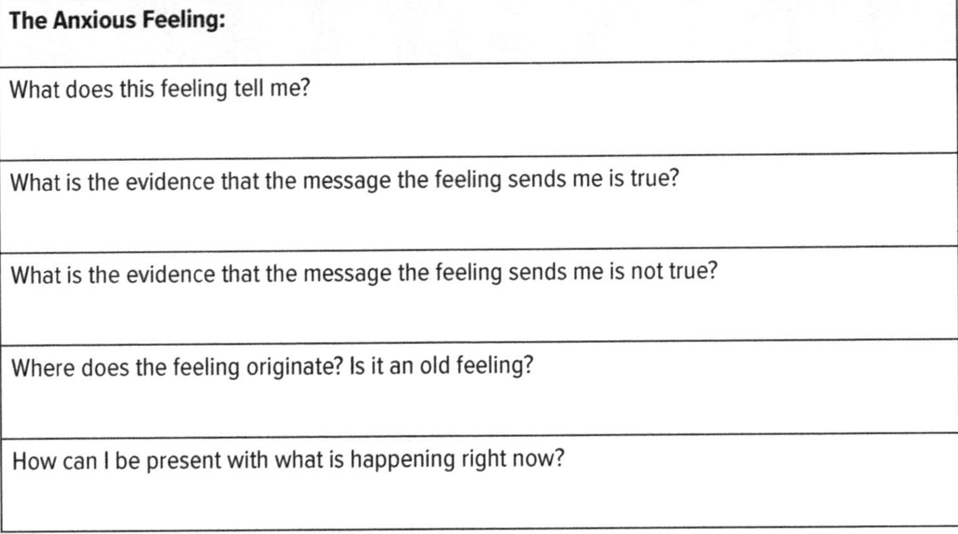

Figure 83

But what about the anxious feeling? The one that does not fit reality?

8. You can still help your client manage the anxious feeling. But it is now with the understanding that the feeling's message is not true, at least not here and now.

9. Summarize what you have done today: You have examined an anxious feeling to see if its message is true here and now. You have used evidence to do so. You have put the anxious feeling in its place, and your feelings have become more present with what is happening.

10. Identify new homework. Give your client this index card:

1.
Does this feeling belong here?

2.
Is the message the feeling
gives me true here and now?

3.
What kind of helpful and
present-oriented action can I take?

Figure 84

Ask your client to take out this index card when she is having a difficult anxious feeling and answer those questions, jotting down some responses on the back of the card. Ask her to bring the card back to your next meeting.

11. Closing: Check in with your client: Does she understand the homework? Are there any barriers to completing it? End your meeting with three calming breaths together.

INTERVENTION 36

From Observation to Action

Practice makes perfect. It is easy for your client to fall back into the old habit of simply believing the message her anxious feelings may tell her. Therefore, the new practice of observing and examining anxious feelings and taking present-oriented and helpful action will have to be practiced. This intervention gives your client another opportunity to practice the sequence observation, examination, action.

Target skill: Planful management of anxious feelings. Insight.

1. Begin with breathing. Ask your client to take three calm breaths with you. Take it slow. When you are done, explore with your client how comfortable this is. In what way is her body now functioning differently?

2. Welcome your client. Ask how the last week went. What went well? What did not go well? Help your client gauge the intensity of her anxious feelings using the scaling arrow. Ask: *In what way are you able to question the messages anxious feelings are sending you? What about this is still difficult?*

3. Identify today's task: Practicing observing and examining anxious feelings, then making plans for helpful and present-oriented action.

   Explain to your client that you understand that changing the long-time habits anxiety has taught her can be difficult, and another round of practice may be a good idea.

4. Review last week's homework: Ask your client to take out the feelings question card. Ask if she used it during the last week. If she did, in what way did this help her? Which question was the most helpful to her?

5. Work on today's task: Practicing the sequence of observing and examining anxious feelings, then taking present-oriented and helpful action. You are going to practice this by first reading the following story to your client, then helping her examine it.

   Jess has suffered from overwhelming anxious feelings for a long time. She does not remember a time when she was not anxious.

   Jess is having a difficult day. She is at the store, feeling anxious in a panicky kind of way. She just has a feeling that something bad is going to happen. She is anxious about people looking at her. She feels anxious about spending her money. She feels anxious about the way she looks. She feels that somehow people are going to find out that she is really just stupid.

   Jess is beginning to shiver and sweat. She is now pacing up and down the store aisles and moving toward the exit. She feels so anxious that she is afraid she is going to die.

6. Begin with observation.

What can your client observe about Jess's anxious feelings? What behaviors does Jess engage in based on her anxious feelings? What is happening to her?

7. Move to examination:

    - Physically, what is happening to Jess?

    - How rational and realistic are her feelings (money, being exposed for being stupid, fear of dying, appearance, the general feeling that something bad is going to happen)?

    - Are her feelings based in reality (shopping experience here and now)?

    - If not, can you speculate where some of these feelings come from?

8. Action planning:

    - What could Jess do about her physical symptoms of anxiety?

    - What reality-based and helpful action can Jess take right there in the store?

    - What things can Jess take with her to plan ahead for these kinds of anxious feelings?

    - What does Jess need to practice in order to prepare for these kinds of anxious feelings?

9. Ask your client: Is it easier to observe and examine someone else's anxious feelings? What would happen if she observed and examined her anxious feelings as if they belonged to someone else? It may just be another way to gain some distance!

10. Summarize the work: Today you have practiced observing and examining anxious feelings. You have used a story to do so. You have then explored how it can be helpful to examine one's own feelings from afar.

11. Identify new homework: Observe an anxious feeling as it occurs. Once she has gained some distance from it, perhaps the next day, she should write down her story and bring it into your next meeting.

12. Closing: Check in with your client. Does she understand the homework? Are there any barriers to completing it? End your meeting with three calming breaths together.

INTERVENTION 37

Anxious Feelings: Exposure 101

Because anxious feelings are unpleasant and can cause a lot of anguish, our clients may often try to avoid them. There are many different ways of doing so: watching television, playing a video game. These may keep the mind busy, but our clients may find that the farther away they try to push their anxious feelings, the more they return in unwanted ways. This intervention asks your client to experience the anxious feeling instead of pushing it away.

Target skill: Tolerating exposure to anxious feelings.

1. Begin with breathing. Ask your client to take three calm breaths with you. Take it slow. When you are done, explore with your client how comfortable this is. In what way is her body now functioning differently?

2. Welcome your client. Ask how the last week went. What went well? What did not go well? Help your client gauge the intensity of her anxious feelings using the scaling arrow.

   Ask: *In what way are you able to question the messages anxious feelings are sending you? What about this is still difficult?*

3. Identify today's task: sitting with and experiencing an anxious feeling, purposefully and fully. Ask your client what she thinks and how she feels about this. Explain that you will help her prepare for the experience.

4. Review last week's homework: Ask your client to read her own anxiety story to you, the one she wrote in response to feeling anxious. Then help her examine her story using the three steps:

   - observation

   - examination

   - planning present-oriented and helpful action

5. Work on today's task: experiencing an anxious feeling without resistance. Begin by educating your client by saying:

   - *Yes, exposure to anxious feelings is distressing.*

   - *The key is to experience the feeling while also regulating body responses in order to avoid a panic response.*

   - *Anxious feelings are likely to increase before they decrease.*

   - *But they will decrease if you keep sitting with them.*

   - *Think of anxious feelings like a wave: The wave will come, but it will also go!*

6. Help your client prepare to experience her anxious feeling. First, help her pick an anxious feeling, one that is not overly distressing. Keep in mind that you want to pick an anxious feeling that matches your client's coping skills. Also remember: Coping is not the same as avoiding. When you cope with an anxious feeling, you are still experiencing it.

7. Help your client identify and practice coping skills that will work for her while experiencing the anxious feeling. Here are some things that may work:

   - Calm breathing.

   - Self-talk such as: *I can sit with this feeling. I feel it without the feeling taking over*.

   - Anything that grounds you here and how: Looking at an object in the room. Feeling the chair or floor. Moving parts of the body.

8. If your client also struggles with dissociation, be sure she is actually present with the anxious feeling. If your client dissociates, you do not really know what she is experiencing. In all likelihood, it is not related to the intended exposure.

   If you suspect that your client is dissociating (staring into space, responding to things that seem unrelated), stop the exposure exercise and assist her with grounding herself in the here and now. Do not continue with exposure until your client has the skills to manage.

9. Engage in exposure. Ask your client to think about the anxious feeling and fully feel it.

   - Name the feeling.

   - Ask your client to welcome the feeling.

   - And stay with the feeling.

   - Tell your client it is OK to talk about the feeling, to share what it feels like.

   - Help your client use any of the coping skills that work for her, but be sure that she stays with the exposure part (unless dissociating).

   - Continue to ask your client to stay with the feeling.

   - Ask your client about her level of anxiety.

   - Help her watch the anxiety level go up and then down.

   - Again, remind your client to stay with the feeling.

   - Even if the anxiety level remains high, your client still gains the experience of being able to tolerate exposure.

   - For many people, however, anxiety will go down after a while.

10. How long should exposure take? Ideally, until your client habituates to the anxious feeling, that is, gets so used to it that her overall anxiety level decreases. If your client's overall anxiety level in response to the anxious feeling does not decrease during the exposure, end the exposure once your client has worked her way through everything outlined under step 9.

11. Help your client reflect on the experience of staying with a feeling instead of avoiding it.

12. Emphasize that though this may have been difficult, she now has the experience of making it through staying with an anxious feeling!

13. Summarize what you have done today: You have prepared and engaged in exposure to an anxious feeling. You have used coping skills to manage the exposure without avoiding the feeling. Your client has now had the experience of making it through!

14. Identify new homework: Ask your client to repeat the experience of exposure to an anxious feeling at home (but only if she did not experience dissociation during the exposure). Be sure to remind her to use her coping skills without avoiding the anxious feeling and to just sit with it. You can give her the following index card to help.

The **anxious** feeling I am going to sit with is:

____

The coping skills I am going to use are:

____

I will now: Just sit with it.

I will not: Be swept away by the anxious feeling or avoid the anxious feeling.

Figure 85

15. Closing: Check in with your client. Does she understand the homework? Are there any barriers to completing it? End your meeting with three calming breaths together.

INTERVENTION 38

Anxious Feelings: Stepping Up Exposure

Our experience with clients tells us that people often try to avoid unpleasant feelings. They may watch television in order not to feel a feeling. Or they may play video games for hours to keep a feeling out of their minds. Avoiding a feeling, of course, does not mean that it is not there. It still lives in the body and will call attention to itself, perhaps through a physical symptom such as a headache. The feeling may be out of mind, but it is still in the body. Acknowledging and managing the feeling is the better way to go.

For most of our clients, exposure to anxiety-provoking behaviors and thoughts happens incrementally, not all at once. When your client learns to be present with anxious feelings, exposure happens in the same way. Start with exposure to a bit of an anxious feeling and move up, step by step, until your client can tolerate being present with very anxious feelings.

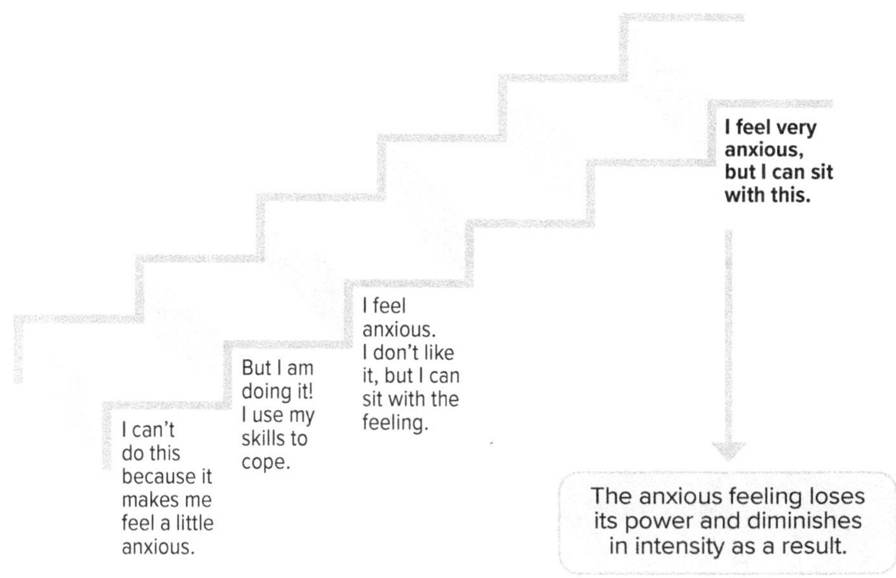

Figure 86

Target skill: Tolerating increased exposure to anxious feelings.

1. Begin with breathing. Ask your client to take three calm breaths with you. Take it slow. When you are done, explore with your client how comfortable this is. In what way is her body now functioning differently?

2. Welcome your client. Ask how the last week went. What went well? What did not go well? Help your client gauge the intensity of her anxious feelings using the scaling arrow.

   Ask: *In what way are you able to question the messages anxious feelings are sending you? What about this is still difficult?*

3. Identify today's task: sitting with increased exposure to anxious feelings. Today your client will sit with moderately anxious feelings. Explain to your client that she is already familiar with the process.

4. Review homework: Ask your client to take out her anxious feelings exposure card. Did she sit with a feeling at home? Did she use her coping skills while doing so? Was she able to manage her discomfort? How did she feel after the home exercise?

5. Work on today's task: Stepping up feelings exposure to a moderately anxious feeling. You may want to show your client the following image again to help her understand the step of exposure.

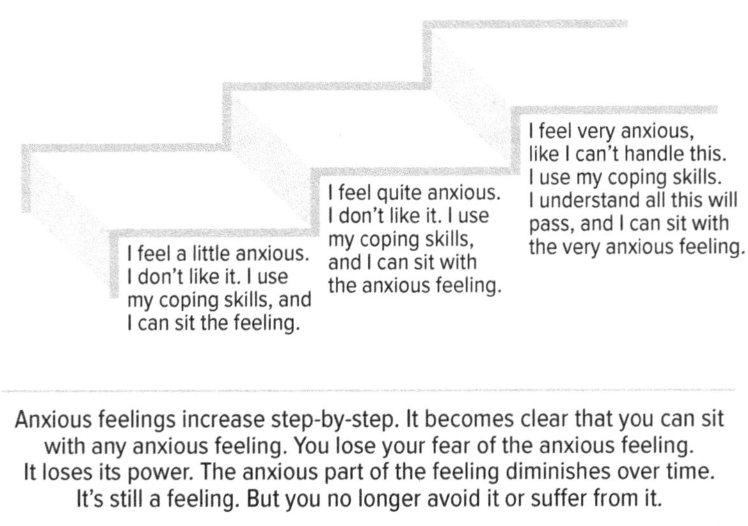

Anxious feelings increase step-by-step. It becomes clear that you can sit with any anxious feeling. You lose your fear of the anxious feeling. It loses its power. The anxious part of the feeling diminishes over time. It's still a feeling. But you no longer avoid it or suffer from it.

Figure 87

6. Work on today's task: experiencing a moderately anxious feeling without resistance (exposure). Begin by educating your client by saying:

   - *Yes, exposure to anxious feelings is distressing.*

   - *The key is to experience the feeling while also regulating body responses in order to avoid a panic response.*

   - *Anxious feelings are likely to increase before they decrease.*

   - *But they will decrease if you keep sitting with them.*

   - *Think of anxious feelings like a wave: The wave will come, but it will also go!*

7. Help your client prepare. First, help your client pick a moderately anxious feeling, one that is not overly distressing. Keep in mind that you want to pick an anxious feeling that matches your client's coping skills. Also remember: Coping is not the same as avoiding. When you cope with an anxious feeling, you are still experiencing it.

8. Help your client identify and practice coping skills that will work for her while experiencing the anxious feeling. Here are some things that may work:

    - Calm breathing.

    - Self-talk such as: "I can sit with this feeling. I can feel it without letting it take over."

    - Anything that grounds you in the here and how: Looking at an object in the room. Feeling the chair or floor. Moving parts of the body.

9. If your client also struggles with dissociation, be sure your client is actually present with the anxious feeling in the here and now. If your client dissociates, you do not really know what she is experiencing. In all likelihood, it is not related to the intended exposure.

    If you suspect that your client is dissociating (staring into space, responding to things that seem unrelated), stop the exposure exercise and assist your client with grounding herself in the here and now. Do not continue with exposure until your client has the skills to manage.

10. Engage in exposure. Ask your client to think about the anxious feeling and fully feel it.

    - Name the feeling.

    - Ask your client to welcome the feeling.

    - And stay with the feeling.

    - Tell your client it is OK to talk about the feeling, to share what it feels like.

    - Help your client use any of the coping skills that work for her, but be sure that she stays with the exposure part (unless dissociating).

    - Continue to ask your client to stay with the feeling.

    - Ask your client about the level of anxiety her anxious feeling induces.

    - Help her watch the anxiety level go up and then down.

    - Again, remind your client to stay with the feeling.

    - Even if the anxiety level remains high, your client still gains the experience of being able to tolerate exposure.

    - For many people, however, anxiety will go down after a while.

11. How long should exposure take? Ideally, until your client habituates to the anxious feeling, that is, gets so used to it that her overall anxiety level decreases. If your client's overall anxiety level in response to the anxious feeling does not decrease during the exposure, end the exposure once your client has worked her way through everything outlined under step 10.

12. Help your client reflect on the experience of staying with the moderately anxious feeling (exposure) instead of avoiding it.

13. Emphasize that though this may have been difficult, she now has the experience of making it through staying with an anxious feeling!

14. Summarize what you have done today: You have prepared and engaged in exposure to a moderately anxious feeling. You have used coping skills to manage the exposure without avoiding the feeling. Your client has now had the experience of making it through!

15. Identify new homework: Ask your client to repeat the experience of exposure to an anxious feeling at home (but only if she did not dissociate during the exposure). Be sure to remind her to use her coping skills without avoiding the anxious feeling and to just sit with it. You can give her the following index card to help.

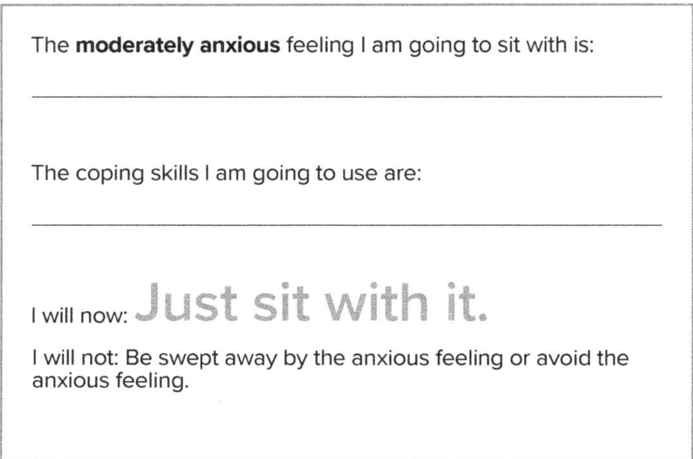

Figure 88

16. Closing: Check in with your client. Does she understand the homework? Are there any barriers to completing it? Does your client have any reservations about sitting with a moderately anxious feeling? Make sure that your client knows her coping skills before moving into exposure to a moderate anxious feeling. End your meeting with three calming breaths together.

INTERVENTION 39

Exposure to Anxious Feelings: Stepping to the Top

Once your client is able to manage sitting with moderately anxious feelings, it is time to take another step. It is important to note that there is nothing different about this step. It too can be managed using the coping skills your client has learned.

Target skill: Tolerating high-level exposure to anxious feelings. Insight.

1. Begin with breathing. Ask your client to take three calm breaths with you. Take it slow. When you are done, explore with your client how comfortable this is. In what way is her body now functioning differently?

2. Welcome your client. Ask how the last week went. What went well? What did not go well? Help your client gauge the intensity of her anxious feelings using the scaling arrow.

   Ask: *In what way are you able to question the messages anxious feelings are sending you? What about this is still difficult?*

3. Identify today's task: sitting with increased exposure to anxious feelings. Today your client will sit with very anxious feelings. Explain that there is nothing different about this step. It can be managed using the coping skills your client has learned. What, then, are very anxious feelings often about?

   - Feeling afraid of dying.

   - Feeling afraid that a loved one will die.

   - Feeling afraid of being all alone, being left.

   - These are just some examples. Your client's deep feelings of anxiety may be triggered by very specific things not on this list.

4. Review homework: Ask your client to take out her anxious feelings exposure card. Did she sit with a feeling at home? Did she use her coping skills while doing so? Was she able to manage her discomfort? How did she feel after the home exercise? Was there any difference in discomfort when stepping up exposure? And if there was, was it manageable?

5. Work on today's task: Experiencing a very anxious feeling without resistance (exposure). Begin by educating your client by saying:

   - *Yes, exposure to very anxious feelings is distressing.*

   - *The key is to experience the feeling while also regulating body responses in order to avoid a panic response.*

   - *Anxious feelings are likely to increase before they decrease.*

   - *But they will decrease if you keep sitting with them.*

   - *Think of anxious feelings like a wave: The wave will come, but it will also go!*

6. Help your client prepare. First, help your client pick a very anxious feeling. This may be the feeling that she has trouble talking about even to you.

7. Help your client identify and practice coping skills that will work for her while experiencing the very anxious feeling. Here are some things that may work:

   - Calm breathing.

   - Self-talk such as: "I can sit with this feeling. I can feel it without letting it take over."

   - Anything that grounds you here and how: Looking at an object in the room. Feeling the chair or floor. Moving parts of the body.

   - Ask: *What are you going to do when you think that you can't handle the feeling anymore?* Making eye contact with you, the provider, can be very grounding.

8. If your client also struggles with dissociation, be sure your client is actually present with the anxious feeling in the here and now. If your client dissociates, you do not really know what she is experiencing. In all likelihood, it is not related to the intended exposure.

   If you suspect that your client is dissociating (staring into space, responding to things that seem unrelated), stop the exposure exercise and assist your client with grounding herself in the here and now. Do not continue with exposure until your client has the skills to manage.

9. Engage in exposure. Ask your client to think about the anxious feeling and fully feel it.

   - Name the feeling.

   - Ask your client to welcome the feeling.

   - And stay with the feeling.

   - Tell your client it is OK to talk about the feeling, to share what it feels like.

   - Help your client use any of the coping skills that work for her, but be sure that she stays with the exposure part (unless dissociating).

   - Continue to ask your client to stay with the feeling.

   - Ask your client about the level of anxiety her anxious feeling induces.

   - Help her watch the anxiety level go up and then down.

   - Again, remind your client to stay with the feeling.

   - Your client may be using eye contact with you to cope. Return the gaze. At that point you must embody neuroception of safety. Understand that if you are afraid of your client's response to exposure, your client will intuitively know this. Embody the message that it is safe to sit with a feeling.

   - Even if the anxiety level remains high, your client still gains the experience of being able to tolerate exposure.

   - For many people, however, anxiety will go down after a while.

10. How long should exposure take? Ideally, until your client habituates to the anxious feeling, that is, gets so used to it that her overall anxiety level decreases. If your client's overall anxiety level in response to the anxious feeling does not decrease during the exposure, end the exposure once your client has worked her way through everything outlined under step 9.

11. Help your client reflect on the experience of staying with the very anxious feeling (exposure) instead of avoiding it.

12. Emphasize that though this may have been difficult, she now has the experience of making it through staying with an anxious feeling!

13. Summarize what you have done today: You have prepared and engaged in exposure to a very anxious feeling. You have used coping skills to manage the exposure without avoiding the feeling. Your client has now had the experience of making it through! This is a tremendous accomplishment, and you should tell your client so.

14. Identify new homework: Ask your client to repeat the experience of exposure to a very anxious feeling at home (but only if she did not experience dissociation during the exposure). Remind her to use her coping skills. You can give her the following index card to help.

The **very anxious** feeling I am going to sit with is:

____

The coping skills I am going to use are:

____

I will now: Just sit with it.

I will not: Be swept away by the anxious feeling or avoid the anxious feeling.

Figure 89

15. Check in with your client: Does she understand the homework? Are there any barriers to completing it? Does your client have any reservations about sitting with a very anxious feeling? Make sure that your client knows her coping skills before moving into exposure to a very anxious feeling. End your meeting with three calming breaths together.

16. Closing: Send your client home with words of encouragement like:

- *Feelings don't have to feel dangerous.*
- *You can sit with them.*
- *You can cope with them.*
- *It just takes practice.*

INTERVENTION 40

Still Feeling Anxious: Managing the Anxious Feelings That Are Left

Many of our clients walk into treatment with the expectation that they will be able to get rid of all of their anxious feelings once and for all. Perhaps they have the unrealistic expectation that they should not ever be anxious. This intervention helps your client return to the idea that anxious feelings are a part of life, that they can serve a purpose. And when they seemingly do not serve a purpose, they can still be felt, examined, and managed.

Target skill: Acceptance and containment of remaining anxious feelings. Insight.

1. Begin with breathing. Ask your client to take three calm breaths with you. Take it slow. When you are done, explore with your client how comfortable this is. In what way is her body now functioning differently?

2. Welcome your client. Ask how the last week went. What went well? What did not go well? Help your client gauge the intensity of her anxious feelings using the scaling arrow. Ask: *In what way are you able to question the messages anxious feelings are sending you? What about this is still difficult?*

3. Identify today's task: Accepting and managing anxious feelings that remain. Briefly explore your client's expectations about her anxious feelings. You can say: *It is understandable that you never want to feel anxious again, but this is not a realistic expectation.*

4. Review homework: Ask your client to take out her anxious feelings exposure card. Did she sit with a feeling at home? Did she use her coping skills? Was she able to manage her discomfort? How did she feel after the home exercise? Was there any difference in discomfort when stepping up exposure? And if there was, was it manageable? If it felt unmanageable, what did your client do to manage in spite of this feeling?

5. Work on today's task: accepting and managing anxious feelings that remain. Begin by congratulating your client for making it through the levels of exposure.

   - Return to psychoeducation: Explain that anxious feelings are built into our bodies to keep us alert to danger and help us survive.

   - We may now feel anxious about things that only seem dangerous, such as perceived rejection by a friend, an insult, or even a poor grade in school.

   - These kinds of anxious feelings can be accepted and managed. Suppressing or avoiding them is unlikely to work.

   - Because suppressing or avoiding anxious feelings that remain or resurface is unlikely to work, we need to care for those feelings with kindness.

   - Why kindness? Kindness is a way of not fueling the flames.

- Kindness is meant to contain anxious feelings. It may be useful to create a container that symbolically holds anxious feelings.

6. Work with your client on creating a container for anxious feelings. Ask:

   What would you like this container to look like? Should it be a box or a bowl? Perhaps an envelope or a basket? How would you like to decorate it?

7. Provide your client with a variety of choices and art materials to create a container for her remaining or resurfacing anxiety. It is important that she make this container her own by decorating it. This will help her with owning and containing her anxious feelings.

8. Once the container is complete, provide your client with a few index cards. Ask her to name at least one remaining anxious feeling and to place it in the container. Help your client explore what this feels like.

9. Review with your client why anxious feelings are placed in the container. They are not placed in the container to be suppressed or avoided, but rather to give them a space to live where they don't interfere with your client's life.

10. Explain that those feelings can then be attended to when it is feasible. They can be felt, accepted, and managed, using the coping skills your client has learned. They no longer pose a threat. They just are.

11. Summarize what you have done so far: You have explored ways in which your client can tolerate exposure to difficult feelings. You have explored the idea of containing any remaining anxious feelings, and your client has created a container to symbolically contain those feelings. She has also used index cards to place those feelings in the container.

12. Leave your client with words of encouragement like:

    - *Whatever feelings are leftover can be contained.*

    - *You can make a choice to contain them and examine them.*

    - *You are in control of what you do with feelings. They are no longer in control of you.*

Working with Phobias

Helping clients manage phobias is fairly straightforward: You are engaging in exposure therapy. Prior sections of this manual have discussed how to use exposure, moving from introspection to real life, and from low-level to high-level exposure.

If your client truly suffers only from a simple phobia and has no other mental health problems, such as anxieties or depression, you may be able to move to a higher level of exposure right away because very little may stand in the way of your client managing the exposure with your help.

Community Mental Health Practice Alert

Many of our clients have more than one mental health diagnosis.

A large number of our clients suffer from chronic exposure to toxic stress, and many of them have also experienced one or more traumatic events. This may make our clients more vulnerable to dissociative experiences.

These kinds of experiences can render exposure ineffective. Exposure is only effective when your client is fully present!

Be sure to carefully assess for the presence of other mental health conditions before engaging in higher-level exposure. If other mental health conditions are present, begin low-level exposure.

Remember: Coping skills first, exposure second.

Exposure therapy does not necessarily include other components of CBT, such as extensive work in the cognitive part of the CBT triad. Your client already knows that her phobia is irrational. She does not need to explore this more than she already has. She just needs the experience of making it through exposure.

Once again, simple body-based coping skills are important. These skills need to be solidly in place before engaging in exposure. Your client needs to be able to ground herself in the here and now using breath and sensory experiences.

Case Example: Jared

Jared is a 32-year-old Hispanic man who is afraid of heights. Jared's fear of heights has become more prominent over the past year after witnessing the death of his best friend in a shooting. This fear is now interfering with his ability to go to work.

Additionally, Jared wakes up drenched in sweat in the middle of the night. He often has nightmares about the shooting he witnessed. He never went back to the location of the shooting and avoids talking to anyone who knew his friend. Sometimes Jared is overcome by intense feelings of sadness for seemingly no reason.

Whenever he has to cross a bridge, Jared begins to sweat and his heart starts to pound. He recently had to move into a new public housing apartment, which is located on the third floor. Jared avoids going anywhere near the windows. This does not leave him much room to live in his small, one-bedroom apartment. Jared has moved his bed into the center of his bedroom.

Jared wonders why his fear of heights is becoming more prominent. He is afraid of losing his job as he is perpetually late trying to get to work avoiding any bridges.

Jared's Phobia in Context

From the story Jared tells his therapist, it has become clear that Jared's phobia of heights is long-standing, but that it is now complicated by the presence of symptoms of PTSD. Hence, Jared is not a good candidate to treat his phobia with exposure therapy only. He will need all the elements of CBT.

- We should begin by assessing which symptoms cause Jared the most functional impairment.

- We should assess which symptoms cause him the most pain.

- We should not engage in higher-level exposure exercises right away, as Jared's long-standing phobia is complicated by the presence of PTSD symptoms.

In this case we would want to begin by educating Jared about the symptoms of both PTSD and his phobia. We would then teach Jared a variety of coping skills for anxious symptoms, as both PTSD and phobias are anxiety disorders. Skill-building will help Jared begin to manage symptoms of his PTSD and his fear of heights.

Once Jared is better able to identify and manage his anxious symptoms, treatment for his phobia can begin. His treatment for the fear of heights would likely follow these steps:

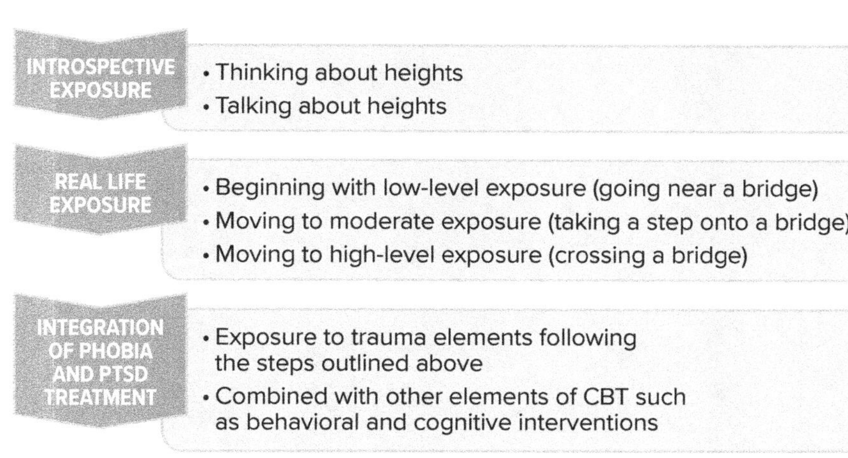
INTROSPECTIVE EXPOSURE
• Thinking about heights
• Talking about heights

REAL LIFE EXPOSURE
• Beginning with low-level exposure (going near a bridge)
• Moving to moderate exposure (taking a step onto a bridge)
• Moving to high-level exposure (crossing a bridge)

INTEGRATION OF PHOBIA AND PTSD TREATMENT
• Exposure to trauma elements following the steps outlined above
• Combined with other elements of CBT such as behavioral and cognitive interventions

Figure 90

Skill Building Interventions

INTERVENTION 41

Breathe Through It

Target skill: Using mindful breathing to cope with anxiety.

1. Welcome your client. Check in with her about her level of anxiety and ability to manage it. How anxious is she today? What is she anxious about? Get to know that flavor of your client's anxiety.

2. Introduce today's task: learning to breathe through anxiety. Explain that this means slowing down her breath to avoid hyperventilating. If your client does not know what hyperventilating is, you may want to demonstrate. Explain that our brains do not work very well when we hyperventilate.

3. Work on today's task: Begin with education. Tell your client that:

   - anxiety often begins with breathing too fast (hyperventilation);

   - slowing down breath can help regulate the body's anxiety response

   - breathing slowly is not meant to avoid anxiety-provoking behaviors, actions, or situations, but rather to manage the anxiety that arises.

4. Demonstrate calm breathing. You can use the "smell the soup, blow on the soup" metaphor. Say this:

   Imagine that there is a bowl of soup in front of you. It smells good. Put your nose close to the bowl and inhale deeply, counting to three.

   Then, breathe out through your mouth, blowing on the soup slowly, counting to ten.

   Show your client how to do this. Demonstrate at least three times. Keep in mind that it is important to breathe out longer than breathing in, but not so long that it becomes uncomfortable. Your client should not be gasping for air when she is done.

5. Now practice this with your client. Say: *Let's do this together. It will take a while to become comfortable with this. Don't worry about doing this perfectly right now, just give it a try.* Practice at least three breaths with your client.

6. Then ask: *What was this like? What was comfortable? What was not?*

7. If necessary, demonstrate and practice together again. If it helps your client, you can put on some relaxation music.

8. Some of our clients are anxious about their bodies or their breath. If your client feels more anxious when learning to slow her breath, start with simply sitting together and listening to some soothing music. Slow and soothing music can also help slow down breath. You can then introduce the idea of consciously slowing down breath.

9. Summarize what you have done today: You have learned that anxiety starts in the body and that slowing down our breathing can calm the body's anxiety response. You have practiced how to slow down breath.

    Assign homework: Ask your client to begin and end each day with three consciously slowed down breaths. Also explain that there is no need to worry about perfection. Ask your client to simply try this without worry. If it helps your client, she may want to end her practice saying: *I can do this. I can get through this.*

10. Closing: Once again explain that anxiety lives in the body and that there are ways to help the body decrease an anxiety response. Check in with your client and answer any questions she may have.

INTERVENTION 42

Skill Building: Opening the Senses, Opening the Mind

This intervention builds on the first mindfulness intervention, which focused on helping your client learn and practice calm breathing. In order to learn this, your client had to become more aware of her breath and her ability to slow it down.

Mindfulness is the full immersion in what you are doing. You are aware what you are doing and observing it nonjudgmentally.

So what is mindful breathing? It's breathing with an awareness of the act of breathing.

What is mindful eating? It's eating with an awareness of the act of eating.

Mindfulness requires openness to sensory experiences and to everything the mind may bring your way.

Target skill: Mindful presence.

1. Begin with breathing. Ask your client to take three deep and calm breaths with you. It may be a good idea to demonstrate this again to set the pace. Then breathe together.

2. Welcome your client. Help her gauge her level of anxiety and her ability to manage it over the past few weeks using the scaling arrow. What went well? What were her most difficult and anxious experiences? Encourage her to just be aware of her difficulties, but in a nonjudgmental way.

3. Identify today's task: Becoming more mindful and opening the senses. Explain that this involves taking in all kinds of experiences, such as things she may see or hear, and doing so without resistance and judgment. What does it mean to take things in without judgment? Here is an example:

   Your client is learning to practice calm breathing. While she is working on this, a fly lands on her arm. She notices it and swats the fly, then immediately feels guilty about not staying on task and interrupting her breathing practice.

   A mindful approach to the dilemma of the fly would be to simply notice the distraction, deal with it, and then go back to practicing the calm breathing. Things happen. Such is life. No need to judge oneself.

4. Review last week's homework: Ask your client if she has practiced mindful breathing. When did she try? How did she feel when she tried this? Review and practice calm breathing together.

5. Work on today's task: becoming mindful and opening the senses.

   Ask your client to look around and describe what she sees in as much detail as she can. Remind her that this is not a competition about noticing detail, just an exercise.

   Listen attentively and comment as appropriate.

Ask your client to sit and listen and describe all the sounds that she is hearing in as much detail as she can. Listen attentively and comment as appropriate.

Now, ask your client to talk about her anxiety-provoking activity or behavior in the same manner. She should simply observe and describe her thoughts and feelings about the activity that she is trying to avoid.

Listen attentively and comment as appropriate. If your client becomes judgmental of herself while she is talking, help her notice this. Don't judge her for judging herself. If your client becomes anxious, ask her to notice that, too.

6. Once you have completed this exercise, help your client reflect on the similarities between the sights and sounds she described and the anxiety-provoking activities. These are all just things that exist. Help your client understand that she can observe her thoughts and behaviors like any other thing.

7. Explore with your client how she can use mindful immersion as a way to calm herself in the face of anxiety. Explain that mindful immersion is not meant to avoid anxiety. On the contrary, it is meant to assist with being fully present with any experience, no matter how unpleasant.

8. Summarize what you have done today: You have worked on understanding mindfulness and mindful immersion in experience. You have applied this idea to sensory experiences such as sight and sound. And you have learned that mindful immersion and observation can also apply to observing one's own avoidance without judgment.

9. Identify new homework: Ask your client to set aside at least two minutes every morning before she begins her day to mindfully immerse herself in all that is around her: What does she see? What does she hear? What does she taste? How about smell? If she notices anxiety passing through her, she should notice that, too.

10. Closing: Today was all about mindfulness. Ask your client to come up with her own definition of mindfulness. If there is anything to clarify, clarify it now. Take notes and save them for your next session.

INTERVENTION 43

Skill Building: Move Through It

Target skill: Using the body to increase tolerance of anxiety.

1. Begin with breathing. Ask your client to calmly breathe with you, taking three breaths. You may want to demonstrate again. Emphasize that perfection is not important and that practice will help.

2. Check in with your client: Use the scaling arrow to help your client gauge her level of anxiety and ability to manage anxious thoughts and behaviors. What went well over the past week? What was your client anxious about but did anyway? How did that experience go? Did she feel accomplished? Or overwhelmed? Explain that both of those feelings are normal responses. If your client did something anxiety provoking, find out how this came about. How did she work through her anxiety? Perhaps she just ignored it? How did that work?

3. Identify today's task: Using motion—in this case, the act of walking—as a backdrop for talking about anxiety-provoking actions. Explain that walking may help with regulating the body's anxiety response.

4. Review last week's homework: Was your client able to practice mindful immersion? How did she feel when she practiced? Pay close attention to your client's body language and facial expressions. If she seems stressed, help her calm herself and explain that it may take time to learn mindful immersion.

5. Work on today's task: "moving through" anxiety-provoking behaviors. Ask your client to pick one behavior from the list of behaviors she is avoiding. Explain that you are going to expose her to the topic of the behavior by talking about it together. Say:

   - *I will not ask you to engage in that behavior today.*

   - *But we will talk about the behavior.*

   - *This will help you get used to the thought of the behavior.*

   - *If you feel anxious about this, this is OK. We will gauge your level of anxiety frequently. If you become overwhelmingly anxious, let me know.*

   Reassure your client that in the event she becomes too anxious, you will take a break and help her regulate together using calm breathing.

6. Explain that you will be walking together while talking. If you are in a small room, you may have to walk in a circle. Explain that being in motion can help her regulate her anxiety without avoiding it.

7. Begin walking together. Ask your client questions about the behavior she is avoiding. Here are some sample questions:

   - *What happens when you* [behavior your client is avoiding]*?*

   - *When is the last time that you* [behavior your client is avoiding]*?*

- *Who is usually with you when you* [behavior your client is avoiding]*?*

- *What is the worst thing that could happen when you* [behavior your client is avoiding]*?*

- *What is the best thing that could happen when you* [behavior your client is avoiding]*?*

8. Be sure to pay attention to your client's body language. If she seems overwhelmed, take a break. Use the scaling arrow to determine together how anxious your client is. If she rates her anxiety at seven or higher, take a break and practice calm breathing together until her anxiety level is below seven.

Figure 91

9. Once your client's anxiety is managed, be sure to move back into the activity of walking and talking about the anxiety-provoking behavior. Go back to asking questions about the behavior until it becomes normal to talk about it. You client is now beginning to habituate to talking about it.

10. Compliment your client on a job well done. Explain that today you have worked together on tolerating talking about the anxiety-provoking behavior in preparation for engaging in it. Explain that walking while talking can be helpful in regulating the body's anxiety response, just like breathing can.

11. Be sure to explain that running while talking does not work because this would increase your client's heart rate and rate of breathing.

12. Summarize what you have done so far: Your client has learned to use walking to help her tolerate exposure to the anxiety-provoking behavior. Walking does not distract, but rather helps to regulate anxious body processes.

13. Assign homework: Ask your client to talk with a friend about her anxiety-provoking behavior. Suggest that the two of them go for a walk together while talking to help regulate your client's anxiety.

14. Be sure to explain that your client should not pick the most anxiety-provoking behavior because this could cause her to feel overwhelmed, which would only reinforce her anxiety.

15. Closing: Summarize again that today was about learning to talk about anxiety-provoking behaviors while moving the body to regulate anxiety. See if your client has any questions and, if she does, answer them.

Skill Building: Change the Scenery

This intervention is designed to help your client change her state of mind when she is anxious about an action, behavior, or event. Anxiety feeds on itself, and every anxious thought seems to call for another. We can interrupt the cycle using a sensory experience, in this case, an image. It is important to note that the sensory experience is not meant to aid in avoidance but to calm the body's stress response.

Target skill: Using sensory experiences to reduce and manage anxiety.

1. Begin with breathing. Welcome your client and ask her to take three calm breaths with you. Take it slow. Pay attention to your client's comfort or discomfort with this. If there is a need, explain again how to slow breath using the "smell the soup, blow on the soup" metaphor.

2. Check in with your client. What went well over the past week? What was she able to do in spite of her anxiety? Did she go to school? Did she give a presentation? Compliment your client on a job well done. Be sure to explain that you understand how difficult it can be to live with anxiety and that you know how hard she is working.

3. Introduce today's task: Changing the scenery when anxiety about an upcoming behavior, action, or event is threatening to take over and lead to avoidance. You can give an example like this:

    Perhaps you have arranged to go on a date. You really want to go, but your anxiety kicks in just as you are about ready to leave. Your anxiety tells you that you should not go, and your anxious thoughts kick in full force, one after another. Your body's stress response is making things more difficult.

    This is the time when your client should change the scenery by looking at a beloved or delightful image.

4. Review last week's homework: Ask your client if she was able to discuss her anxiety-provoking behavior with a friend while walking together. Did walking help soothe her anxiety? What was her friend's response? How did she feel after walking and talking with her friend? Does she think the experience may be worth repeating?

5. Work on today's task: Changing the scenery when anxiety takes over and there is a danger she may avoid an upcoming behavior.

    - Explain that changing the scenery is different from avoidance. It simply resets her body's stress response to a calmer state so that she can go back to what she was going to do.

    - Ask your client to name a place, person, image, or experience that always gives her a sense of calm. Here are some examples:

        - a puppy
        - a beautiful lake

- a smiling baby

- flowers

- a family picture

6. Be sure to spend enough time to figure out what truly gives your client a sense of calm. Pay close attention to her body language and facial expressions. When you see your client's face and body settle, you are probably on the right track. Keep in mind that what calms a person can be very specific.

7. Stay away from using video games to create a sense of calm. Your client is not truly calm when she is gaming. In most cases gaming is more numbing than awakening.

8. Spend some time looking for an image of your client's calming prompt. Perhaps she already has the perfect photograph with her. There are many beautiful images you can find on the Internet that may work. Just search for "cute animals" and you will find a multitude of images that should make you and your client smile.

9. Look at the image together. Ask your client to describe it to you. What kind of feeling does she get when she looks at it? Help your client fully immerse herself in the image!

10. If you can, print out the image or help your client find an easy way to access it on her phone by writing down the web address.

11. Take out an index card and either glue the image on the card or write the web address for the image on the card.

12. Review what you have done today: Your client has learned to change the scenery in preparation for engaging in an anxiety-provoking behavior. Explain again that changing the scenery can help reset the body's stress response system. This, in turn, will help her not to avoid the activity.

13. Assign homework: Give your client the index card with the calming image or web address. Ask her to carry it with her and look at it for a minute at the beginning of every day. She should then carry it with her and take it out when anxiety about a behavior threatens to take over. Ask her to fully immerse herself in the image for a minute or two and then return to her task at hand. She can repeat use of the calming image as needed and perhaps the image will embed itself in her memory after a while and just be with her wherever she goes.

14. Closing: Ask your client if she has any questions. If she does, answer them. Wish her well on her journey of learning to calm her mind and body's stress response.

INTERVENTION 45

Skill Building: Firmly Grounded

This intervention will help your client feel firmly grounded where she is, using her sense of touch to help her stay connected in the present.

Target skill: Using touch and the body to increase tolerance of anxiety.

1. Begin with breathing. Welcome your client and ask her to take three calm breaths with you. Take it slow. Pay attention to your client's comfort or discomfort with this. If there is a need, explain again how to slow breath using the "smell the soup, blow on the soup" metaphor.

2. Check in with your client. What went well over the past week? What was she able to do in spite of her anxiety? Did she go to school? Did she give a presentation? Compliment your client on a job well done. Be sure to explain that you understand how difficult it can be to live with anxiety and that you know how hard she is working.

3. Introduce today's task: being firmly grounded in the present by using the body. You can say something like this: *You will learn to stay present by feeling the ground underneath your feet or the chair behind your back.*

4. Review last week's homework: Ask your client about her calming card. Did she use it to connect with calming images? What impact did this have on her? Was there one image that was particularly helpful? If there was, ask your client to show it to you and then describe it to you to recreate the sense of calm.

5. Work on today's task: Ask your client to find a comfortable position to sit in. She can sit in a chair. She could also sit on the ground leaning against the wall. Some clients may prefer to lie flat on the ground (if your office is big enough to allow this). Look at where your client's body is making contact with the ground or other surface.

    Ask your client to take three calming breaths with you. Your client may want to close her eyes during this intervention, but this is not necessary.

    Then ask her to feel the ground underneath her feet. Speak slowly when you are asking her to do so. Begin with asking her to feel the ground underneath her left foot, then her right foot, taking a breath in between.

    Then move on to other parts of the body that are touching a surface. Say: *Feel the chair behind your back. Feel how it supports you and carries you. Feel your arms resting on your legs.* And so forth.

    As you are doing this, breathe calmly and continue to use a soothing voice.

    Emphasize that your client is supported by her environment.

    If your client shifts positions during the exercise, this is OK. Respond to her shift of position by exploring how she is now supported in a different way.

6. Summarize what you have done so far: You have explored and felt the ways in which your client is supported by her environment. You have helped your client create a sense of calm through feeling the ways in which she is supported and carried by her environment.

7. Assign new homework: Ask your client to practice feeling supported once every day during the next week. Ask her to pick a chair or other spot to sit and describe it to you and to also pick a time when she will engage in this activity.

8. Closing: Ask your client if she has any questions. If she does, answer them. Wish her well on her journey of learning to calm her mind and body's stress response.

Exposure Interventions

INTERVENTION 46

Facing Anxiety: Beginning Exposure

Your client has now learned (and hopefully mastered) basic skills for calming her mind and body. Keep in mind that moving into exposure to higher levels of anxiety will only work if your client has learned and practiced her calming skills. She needs to be somewhat comfortable with using calming skills, and they should eventually become second nature.

While learning and practicing calming skills, your client has also been exposed to thoughts about anxiety-provoking behaviors. CBT calls this *introspective exposure* (as opposed to real-life, *in vivo* exposure. Keep in mind that exposure should raise your client's anxiety somewhat, but not so much that she becomes completely overwhelmed and moves into a fight/flight/freeze response, in which case she would be unable to learn anxiety-management skills.

Target skill: Tolerating exposure to phobic focus. Coping.

1. Begin with breathing. Ask your client to take three calm breaths with you. Take it slow. When you are done, explore with your client how comfortable she has become with using breath to calm herself. Ask: Is this becoming second nature? Does she practice calm breathing every day? If she does not, encourage her to do so at the beginning and end of every day.

2. Introduce today's task: Beginning real exposure to the feared behavior or content.

   Explain that in order to manage a phobia it will be necessary to face the phobic behavior or content. You may want to go back to the behavior baseline chart (see Intervention 2). What behaviors does your client avoid? Which real activity is she willing to try?

3. Ask your client to rate her phobias on a scale from 1-3, with one being a little anxiety provoking and 3 being very anxiety provoking.

4. Once she has done so, ask her to pick a behavior rated 1. You can explain that in order to be successful, it is best to begin with an anxiety-provoking behavior that evokes some anxiety, but not too much.

5. Once she has chosen an activity, help your client make a plan for engaging in it. The plan could look something like this:

Anxiety Provoking Behavior		
When I will engage in this behavior:	Day:	Time
What I will do if my anxiety level goes up:		
1.		
2.		
3.		
4.		

Figure 92

6. Make sure that your client's plan is very specific. Your client should pick specific and workable skills to manage her anxiety. These are skills she is comfortable with and that have become close to second nature.

7. Make a contingency plan: Let's pretend that your client engages in the anxiety-provoking behavior and goes through all of her coping skills, but none of them seem to work. What should your client do then?

   Return to the idea of mindful immersion. Explain that it is possible to observe and experience anxiety without running with it. Ask your client to just let the anxiety be. It is there. It comes, but it also goes. Your client should, if at all possible, go through with the planned anxiety-provoking experience because this is the only way she can learn that anxiety can be managed.

   If your client cannot succeed by herself, she may need to be coached through the experience. Sometimes it may be necessary for you to accompany your client into the community and walk her through the process of engaging in an anxiety-provoking behavior. Talk with your supervisor and make a plan that ensures everyone's confidentiality.

   There are situations in which your client may need to enlist a friend as a coach. Clearly, if going out on a date is an anxiety-provoking behavior, you cannot go. and you should talk about who might be able to coach her through the experience.

8. Summarize what you have done today: You have made a plan for your client to engage in an anxiety-provoking behavior in real life. You have also chosen calming and coping skills she can use to make it through.

9. Assign new homework: You know what is coming. Your client will engage in the anxiety-provoking behavior in real life. Ask her to take a few notes about how it went and bring those notes to your next meeting.

10. Closing: Send your client home with a few words of support. Say something like:

You have come a long way, and it is time to put those skills you have learned into practice. You can do this. You can [activity your client can now engage in], *even if it causes you to be anxious. You can manage this.*

INTERVENTION 47

Facing Anxiety: Stepping Up Exposure

Your client should move on to this intervention is she has successfully engaged in the last intervention. If your client did not complete her homework, you should continue to work on completing the exposure intervention until she does. Your client needs the experience of successfully completing a behavior in spite of anxiety. There has to be exposure in order to be successful.

What does success mean? Success means that your client was able to manage her anxiety. It does not mean that your client did not become anxious. Here is what success looks like:

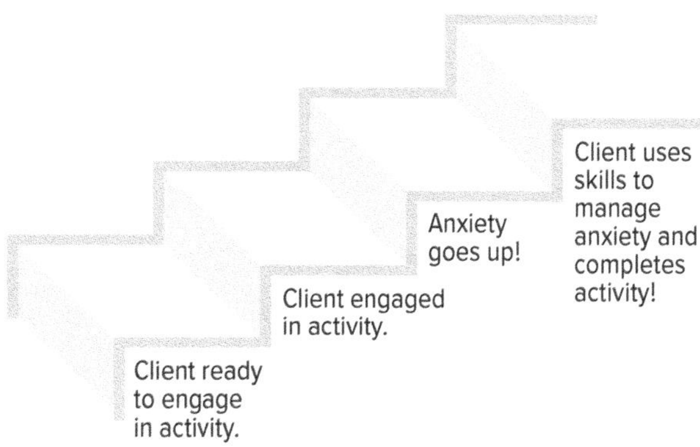

Figure 93

The intervention is successful if your client engages in the anxiety-provoking activity, uses her coping skills, and completes the activity.

Target skill: Tolerating increased exposure to phobic focus. Coping.

1. Begin with breathing. Ask your client to take three calm breaths with you. Take it slow. When you are done, explore with your client how comfortable she has become with using breath to calm herself. Ask: Is this becoming second nature? Does she practice calm breathing every day? If she does not, encourage her to do so at the beginning and end of every day.

2. Identify today's task: stepping up exposure. Congratulate your client on making it through the first intervention in spite of her anxiety. Say: *Now that you know it is possible to be anxious about something and do it anyway, we can move on to another difficult behavior.*

3. Review last week's homework: Inquire about your client engaging in the anxiety-provoking behavior in real life. How difficult was this? You can use the scaling arrow to help your client gauge her level of anxiety before and during the activity. You should also ask what her level of anxiety was after the activity.

Figure 94

4. Work on today's task: Begin by explaining that if mild anxiety can be managed by using coping skills, then more anxiety can be managed, too. You can use the following image to help your client understand how exposure works.

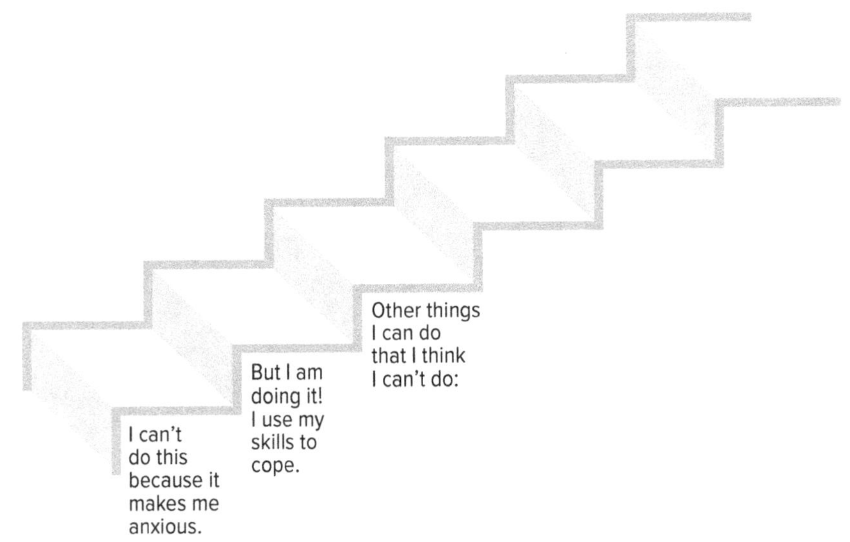

Figure 95

Help your client wonder out loud, like this:

If I can _________ , then I can probably _________.

Be sure to explain to your client that the next step should be one step up. It is best not to go three steps up because you want your client to be successful, and this means that she can manage her anxiety.

5. Ask your client to clearly identify the next step. This should be an activity or behavior that evokes moderate anxiety (a 2 on a scale from 1-3). Ask your client to write that step on the step chart.

6. Help your client explore how she feels about taking the step. It is likely that your client becomes anxious. Help your client manage the anxiety and talk

about the proposed next step anyway. You are engaging in exposure by thinking about the behavior. This is a great opportunity to practice skills.

7. Now plan ahead using the following chart:

Anxiety Provoking Behavior		
When I will engage in this behavior:	Day:	Time
What I will do if my anxiety level goes up:		
1.		
2.		
3.		
4.		

Figure 96

Add as many coping skills as you can to the chart. Because this behavior is predicted to cause moderate anxiety, you may need more or different coping skills. Help your client be fully prepared by asking:

What if _________ happens?

8. Reinforce the idea that the activity must be completed. Avoidance cannot be an option, as this would reinforce the faulty idea that anxiety can't be managed!

9. Summarize today's work: You have taken one step up on the steps of anxiety-provoking behaviors. You have first talked about the behavior (introspective exposure). You have then identified a number of coping skills your client can use when engaging in the activity in real life. Your client has completed a coping chart to carry with her, as it is easy to forget things when under stress.

10. Assign homework: Send the chart home with your client. Ask your client to complete the identified behavior using the coping skills.

11. Closing: Address any reluctance before your client leaves. Reinforce that anxiety is unsettling but will pass. You can use the metaphor of anxiety as a con man: Anxiety cons you into believing that you have to avoid certain behaviors, but it's just not true!

INTERVENTION 48

Facing Anxiety: Stepping to the Top

The following intervention is, in essence, a repetition. You will help your client (a) identify a behavior that is very anxiety provoking, (b) explore feelings and thoughts related to that behavior, (c) prepare your client to engage in the behavior by identifying additional coping skills, and (d) ask your client to engage in the behavior in the real world.

You should only proceed to the top if your client was able to manage her anxiety and engage in the behavior causing her to have moderate anxiety.

The 1-3 rating scale is a suggestion. You can stretch this scale if needed. You client may need a scale from 1-5. This is OK.

Target skill: Tolerating high-level exposure to phobic focus. Coping. Insight.

1.   Begin with breathing. Ask your client to take three calm breaths with you. Take it slow. When you are done, explore with your client how comfortable she has become with using breath to calm herself. Ask: Is this becoming second nature? Does she practice calm breathing every day? If she does not, encourage her to do so at the beginning and end of every day.

2.   Identify today's task: making it to the top of the stairs. Explain that this may seem like a tall order, but that it really is not. Your client already knows how to use coping skills for anxiety. Taking one more step up can be scary, but it is really no different than the other steps.

3.   Review last week's homework: Ask your client to discuss the moderately anxiety-provoking behavior with you. Did she engage in the behavior in spite of her anxiety? Which one of her coping skills worked best? (Make a note of that one, as you should use it for today's intervention.) Which one did not help her? Was there a point at which she almost gave up? What kept her going?

     If your client did not complete the activity, find out why. Did her faulty thoughts get to her? Normalize failure as part of learning. Find out what went wrong, identify additional coping skills, and repeat the intervention.

4.   Work on today's task: making it to the top of the stairs.

     Begin by asking your client what behaviors and activities are most anxiety provoking. Try to get a feeling for the flavor of your client's anxiety. Is it mostly related to social interactions? Or perhaps feelings of inadequacy? Or fear of rejection? Help your client understand the themes of her anxieties.

     While you are exploring the themes and flavors of her most anxiety-provoking behaviors, you are once again engaging in introspective exposure. Help your client monitor her anxiety level using the scaling arrow. If necessary, move into using coping skills for anxiety. Generally speaking, once anxiety moves past the number 7 (on a scale from 1-10), it is a good idea to use coping skills to dial down anxiety.

Keep in mind coping skills are not a means of avoidance. Once anxiety is down again, resume talking about the anxiety-provoking behavior.

Once you have explored and managed anxiety while talking about the behavior (introspective exposure), move into planning to engaging in the behavior in real life.

Once again, use the following chart to plan:

Anxiety Provoking Behavior		
When I will engage in this behavior:	Day:	Time
What I will do if my anxiety level goes up:		
1.		
2.		
3.		
4.		

Figure 97

Be sure to only list tried-and-true coping skills on the chart. If a coping skill did not work well for a moderately anxiety-provoking behavior, do not include it.

5. Summarize what you have done so far. You have identified a very anxiety-provoking behavior and explored it (introspective exposure). You have then made a plan to engage in the behavior and have identified coping skills that fit the situation.

6. Now is a good time to remind your client that anxiety is the body's response to threats. More often than not, the threat is perceived, not real, meaning anxiety, the great con man, is tricking her into believing that she can't do something. It may be anxiety provoking, but it is definitely doable.

7. Assign homework: Send your client home with the chart and ask her to engage in the anxiety-provoking activity in real life. Remind her that she has the skills to succeed.

8. Closing: Be sure to ask about any barriers that might stand in the way of homework completion. Here are some typical barriers:

    - Your client is saying yes but is still really scared to complete the homework.

    - Your client forgets about homework.

    - Your client does not believe that exposure can work for her.

Address any questions or concerns your client may have in order to make sure she will complete the homework.

INTERVENTION 49

Working with Failure

This intervention addresses the need to work with failure. You can address perceived failure by reframing it as part of the learning process. You can also find success within failure. If your client completed part of the exposure exercises, then she was partly successful. She took a step up the stairs, there may be another step ahead.

Target skill: Acceptance. Reframing perceived failure as opportunity to practice. Coping with phobias.

1. Begin with breathing. Ask your client to take three calm breaths with you. Take it slow. When you are done, explore with your client how comfortable she has become with using breath to calm herself. Ask: Is this becoming second nature? Does she practice calm breathing every day? If she does not, encourage her to do so at the beginning and end of every day.

2. Check in with your client: How does she feel about exposing herself to anxiety-provoking thoughts and behaviors? Is she beginning to gain a sense that anxiety is manageable? That she can walk through the storm and find calm on the other side?

3. Review homework. You can ask:

    - *Did you engage in the anxiety-provoking behavior?*

    - *What did it feel like?*

    - *How were you able to regulate anxious body processes?*

   Be sure to highlight any successes. Perhaps your client was successful just once. This is success. It means she has the skills to do it again. Remind her that practice will help.

4. Identify today's task: working with failure.

    - Help your client identify situations in which she thought she failed. Perhaps she did not fully complete an assignment or was too scared to tell you she did not succeed.

    - Listen to your client with compassion.

    - Identify thinking errors such as, "I failed, therefore I am a failure," or, "I failed and my therapist thinks I am a failure/my therapist hates me."

    - Explain that you will work on integrating perceived failure into treatment.

    - Explain that failure is to be expected. It is a normal part of life. So is success.

5. Review last week's homework: Ask about your client's experience of engaging in the very anxiety-provoking behavior. Listen carefully as your client tells the story. Is she telling you what happened with pride? Is the experience of talking to you about this anxiety provoking? Pay attention to your

client's body language and facial expressions. Use your breath and posture to help your client regulate.

If your client perceived that she has failed in some way, explore this with her and reframe perceived failure as an opportunity to learn more. If your client avoided the activity, explore the idea of anxiety having a friend: the big bad bully of avoidance. The big bad bully of avoidance tells you that everything will be better if you just don't engage in anything that provokes anxiety. The trouble with this, of course, is that the bully is lying.

6. Work on today's task: working with failure using the following worksheet:

Things I can say to the failure/avoidance bully:
You are a liar!
. . .

Things I can do about the failure/avoidance bully:
Anticipate that he will show up.
Be prepared for his lies.
. . .

How I can welcome the failure/avoidance bully without believing his message:
Listen, but not believe his words . . .
. . .

Figure 99

What you are trying to do, once again, is help your client understand that the avoidance bully has no power. She does not have to listen to him (you are now working within the cognitive element of the triad). If she does listen to him, she could listen with compassion. If your client suggests that she could just run away from the failure bully, say this:

> **Bullies usually chase you. How about facing instead of running?**

Here are ways of listening to the failure bully with compassion:

- Ask the bully what made him so very pessimistic. What has happened to him?
- Teach the bully calm breathing.
- Ask the bully if he is lonely.
- Ask the bully if he needs a friend.

7. Help your client complete the worksheet using Socratic questions. Once your client has completed that worksheet, suggest that it is possible to embrace perceived failure as part of the process of learning to manage anxious thoughts, feelings, and behaviors. Ask:

   - *How can you embrace failure as a part of the process of managing anxiety?*
   - *In what way can failure be helpful?*
   - *How can you be kind to failure?*
   - *How can you be kind to yourself when you perceive that you have failed?*

8. Summarize what you have done together today:

   - You have explored the many ways in which failure can be like a bully.
   - You identified how your client can face the bully of avoidance and embrace perceived failure as part of the process of learning to manage anxiety.

9. Identify new homework: Send your client home with the failure/avoidance bully worksheet. Ask her to use the different ways she has identified to talk back to the bully. If a specific way of responding to the bully worked, she

should use a highlighter to mark it. Ask her to bring the worksheet back to your next meeting.

10. Closing: Before your client leaves, acknowledge how powerful bully messages can be. But this does not mean that they are true. You can say this: If you know that a dish is poisoned, you will not eat it. Bully messages are poison—don't take them in!

Appendix: Selected Figures

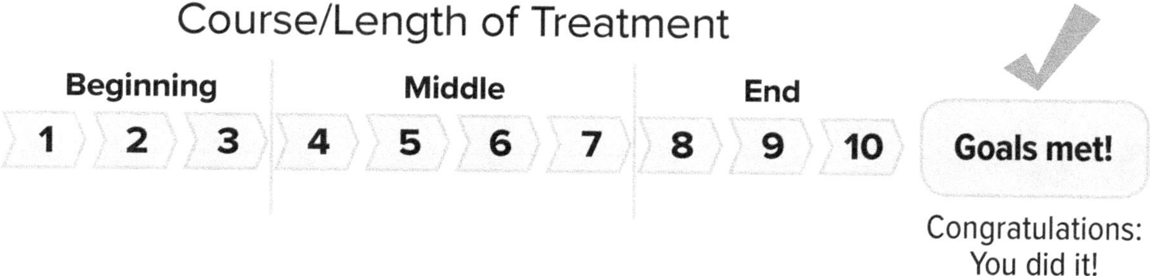

Figure 12

CBT Session Structure
Check-In
Identify Today's Task
Homework Review
Work on Today's Task
Summarize the Work
Identify New Homework
Closing

	Mon	Tue	Wed	Thu	Fri	Sat	Sun
Hours in bed							
Hours of TV							

Figure 13

	Mon	Tue	Wed	Thu	Fri	Sat	Sun
Contacted friend/family member X							

Figure 14

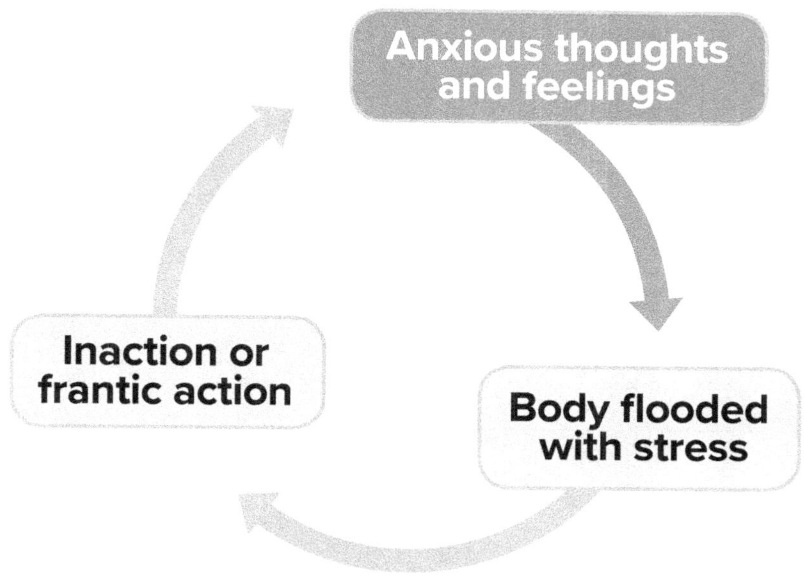

Figure 15

	Mon	Tue	Wed	Thu	Fri	Sat	Sun
Morning							
Afternoon							
Evening							

Figure 17

Automatic Thought	Evidence for AT	Evidence against AT

Figure 19

From *Treating Anxiety Using Cognitive Behavioral Therapy Skills and Interventions*. © OhioGuidestone. Owners of this book are granted permission to reproduce pages for use with their clients.

Nonsense Thought	Anxious Thought	(Overly) Optimistic Thought	Realistic Thought

Figure 21

From *Treating Anxiety Using Cognitive Behavioral Therapy Skills and Interventions*. © OhioGuidestone. Owners of this book are granted permission to reproduce pages for use with their clients.

Figure 22

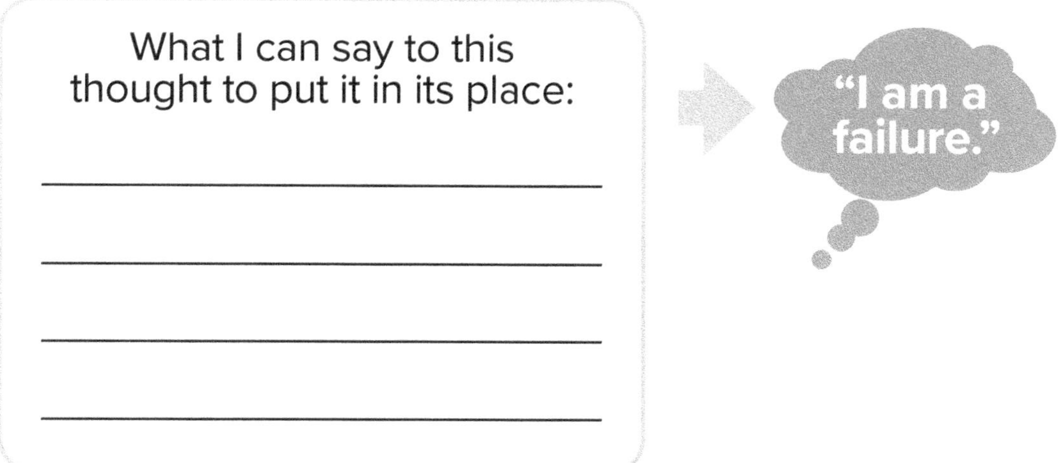

Figure 23

Figure 24

Figure 26

Figure 27

Figure 28

Things I want to ask my anxious thoughts/tell my anxious thoughts:
You don't rule me.
What are you trying to tell me?
Why should I listen to you?

Figure 29

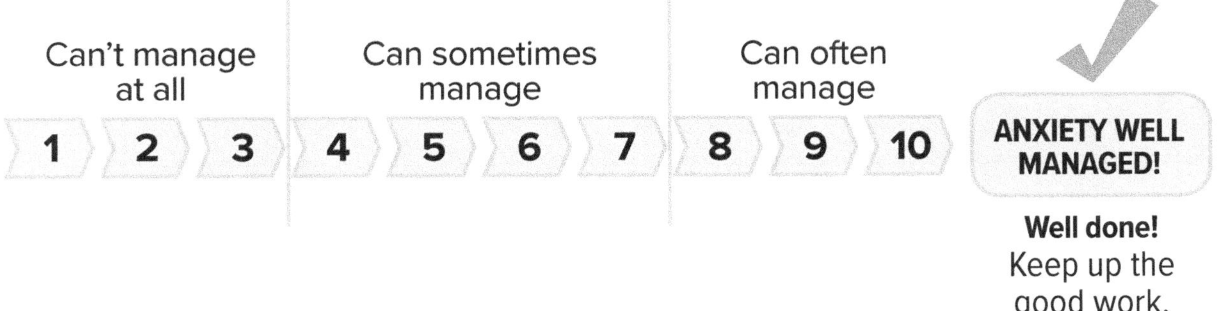

Figure 30

	Thought I am going to sit with:	Daily time:	Done
Mon			
Tue			
Wed			
Thu			
Fri			
Sat			
Sun			

Figure 31

Figure 33

Automatic Thought	Evidence for AT	Evidence against AT

Figure 34

This is just a thought.

It will pass.

I think it now, but I can let it go.

I am letting this thought go.

And if it returns, I will let it go again.

It is just a thought.

Figure 35

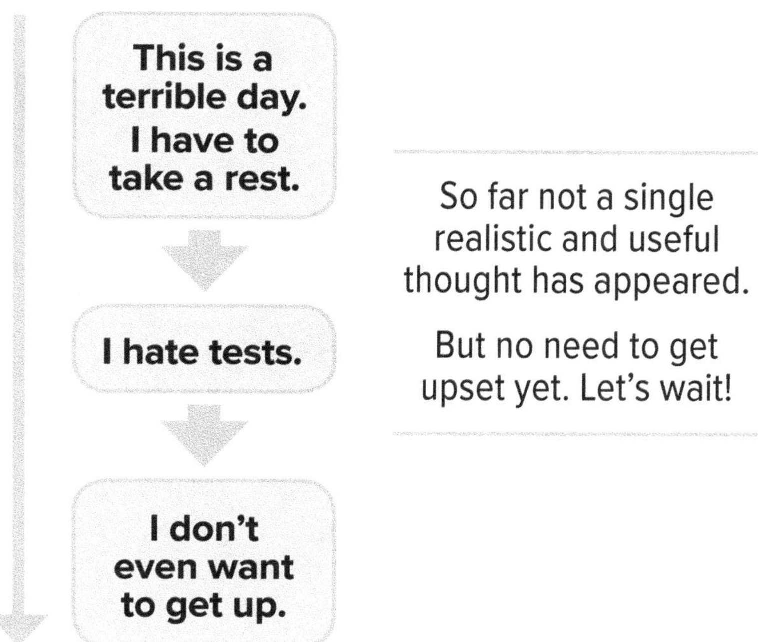

Figure 36

Figure 37

Figure 39

Particularly Pesky Anxious Thought
Thoughts that feed anxiety:
Thoughts that don't feed anxiety:

Figure 40

Figure 43

Figure 44

Figure 45

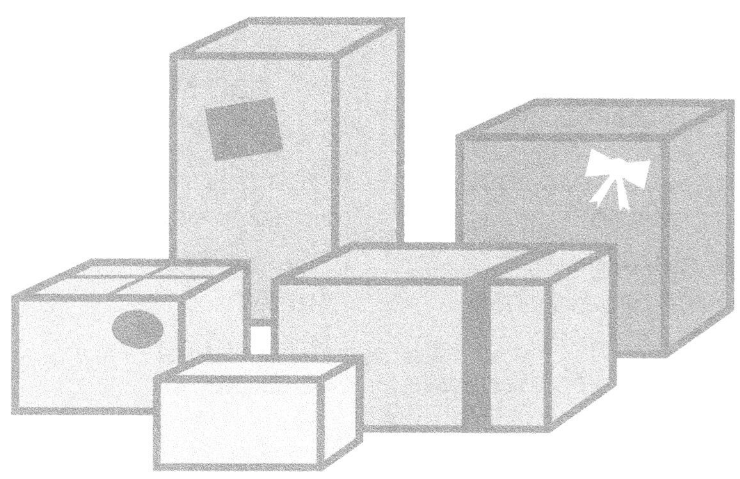

Figure 46

Figure 47

NO ANXIETY	JUST ENOUGH ANXIETY	TOO MUCH ANXIETY
• All seems well. • No new skills are learned.	• Anxiety response activated. • Fight/Flight/ Freeze response not activated. • Learning to manage anxiety is possible.	• Fight/Flight/ Freeze response. • Focused on survival. • No learning is possible.

Figure 49

Figure 50

Things I avoid because they make me feel anxious	Things I do to avoid the thing I am anxious about	How much time I spend avoiding the things that make me anxious

Figure 51

Voice telling you:

Figure 53

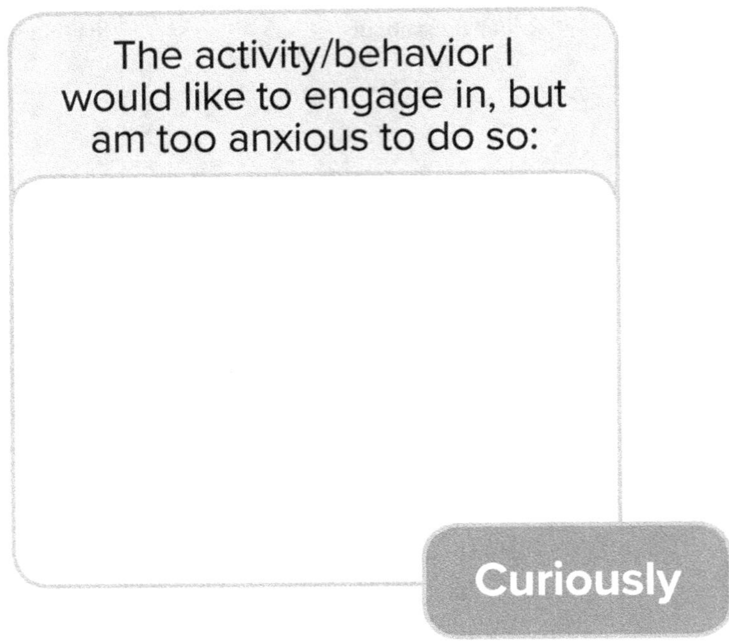

Figure 54

From *Treating Anxiety Using Cognitive Behavioral Therapy Skills and Interventions.* © OhioGuidestone. Owners of this book are granted permission to reproduce pages for use with their clients.

Anxiety Provoking Behavior		
When I will engage in this behavior:	Day:	Time
What I will do if my anxiety level goes up:		
1.		
2.		
3.		
4.		

Figure 55

From *Treating Anxiety Using Cognitive Behavioral Therapy Skills and Interventions.* © OhioGuidestone. Owners of this book are granted permission to reproduce pages for use with their clients.

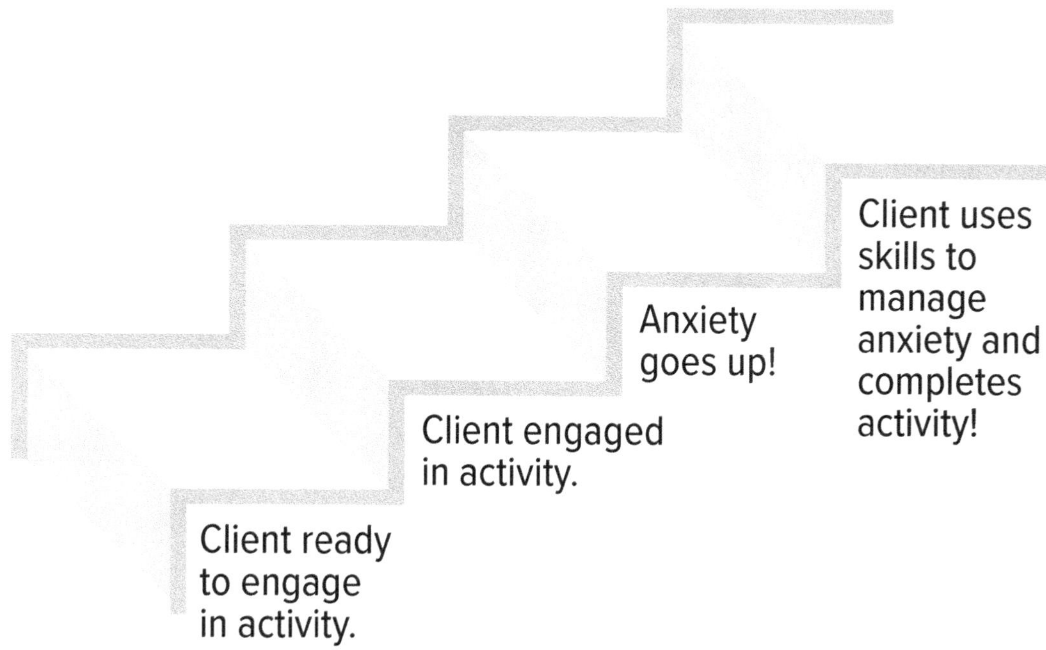

Figure 56

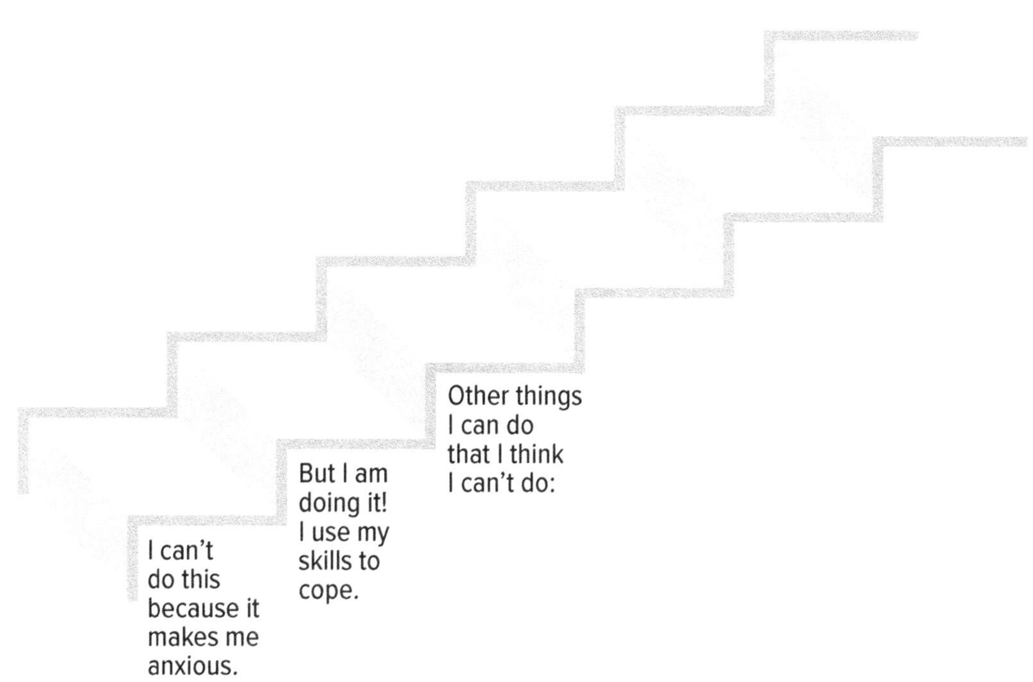

Figure 58

Things I can say to the failure/avoidance bully:
You are a liar!

Things I can do about the failure/avoidance bully:
Anticipate that he will show up.
Be prepared for his lies.
. . .

How I can welcome the failure/avoidance bully without believing his message:
Listen, but not believe his words . . .

Figure 62

Figure 63

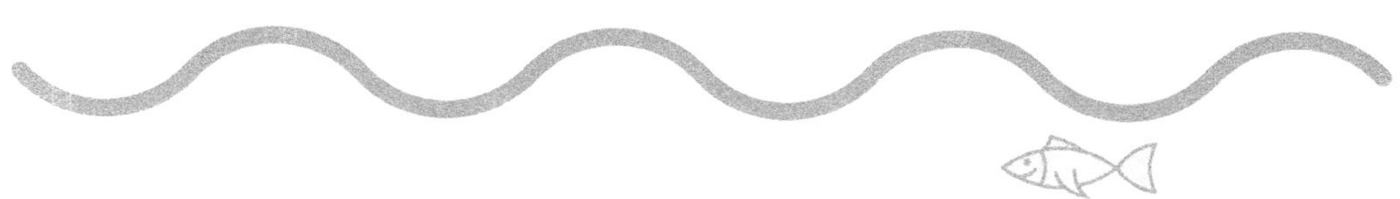

Figure 64

Figure 65

Riding the waves: Draw the "waves" for every day
Monday:
Tuesday:
Wednesday:
Thursday:
Friday:
Saturday:
Sunday:

Figure 66

Figure 67

Figure 68

Figure 69

From *Treating Anxiety Using Cognitive Behavioral Therapy Skills and Interventions*. © OhioGuidestone. Owners of this book are granted permission to reproduce pages for use with their clients.

Figure 70

From *Treating Anxiety Using Cognitive Behavioral Therapy Skills and Interventions*. © OhioGuidestone. Owners of this book are granted permission to reproduce pages for use with their clients.

Figure 72

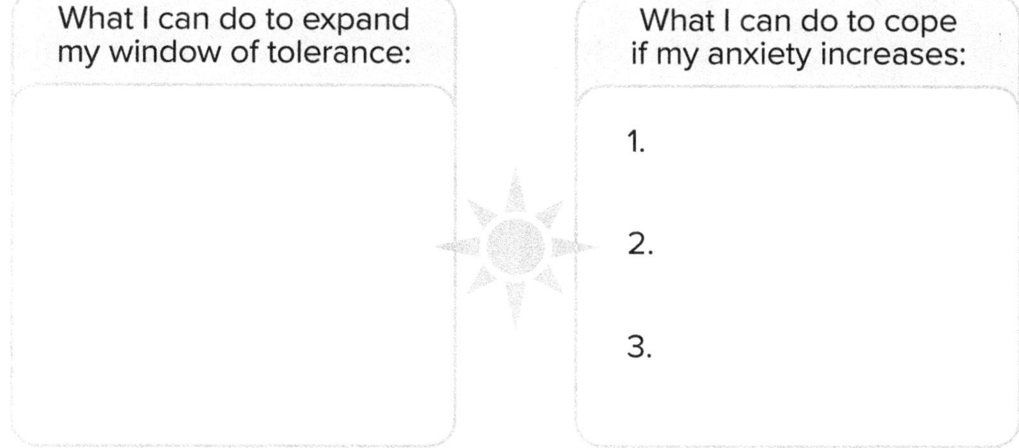

Figure 74

Figure 77

Figure 79

Mindful preparation for anxious feelings
Breathe:
Sing:
Talk to a friend:

Figure 81

The Anxious Feeling:
What does this feeling tell me?
What is the evidence that the message the feeling sends me is true?
What is the evidence that the message the feeling sends me is not true?
Where does the feeling originate? Is it an old feeling?
How can I be present with what is happening right now?

Figure 82

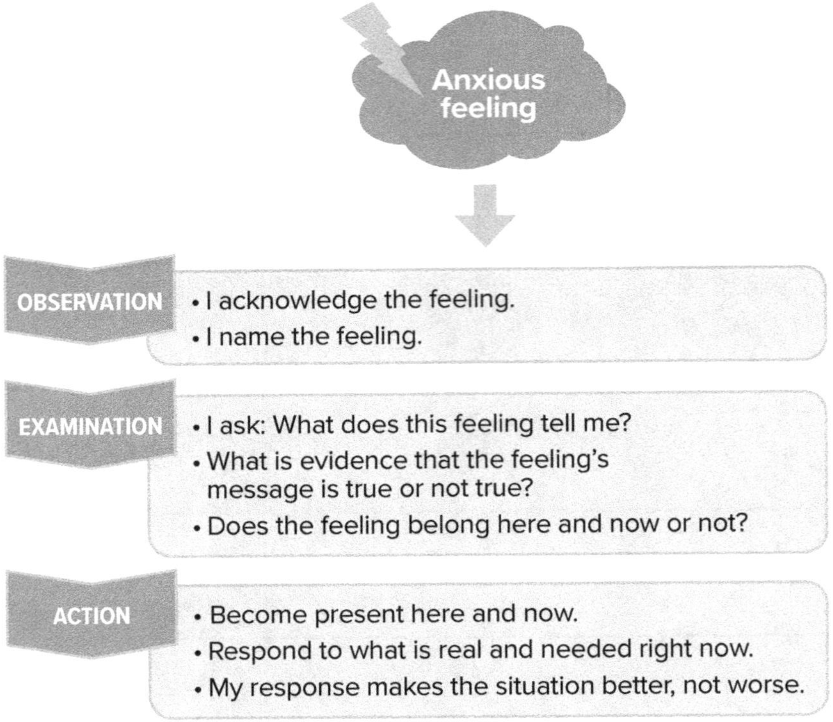

Figure 83

From *Treating Anxiety Using Cognitive Behavioral Therapy Skills and Interventions.* © OhioGuidestone. Owners of this book are granted permission to reproduce pages for use with their clients.

1.
Does this feeling belong here?

2.
Is the message the feeling
gives me true here and now?

3.
What kind of helpful and
present-oriented action can I take?

Figure 84

The **anxious** feeling I am going to sit with is:

____

The coping skills I am going to use are:

____

I will now: Just sit with it.

I will not: Be swept away by the anxious feeling or avoid the anxious feeling.

Figure 85

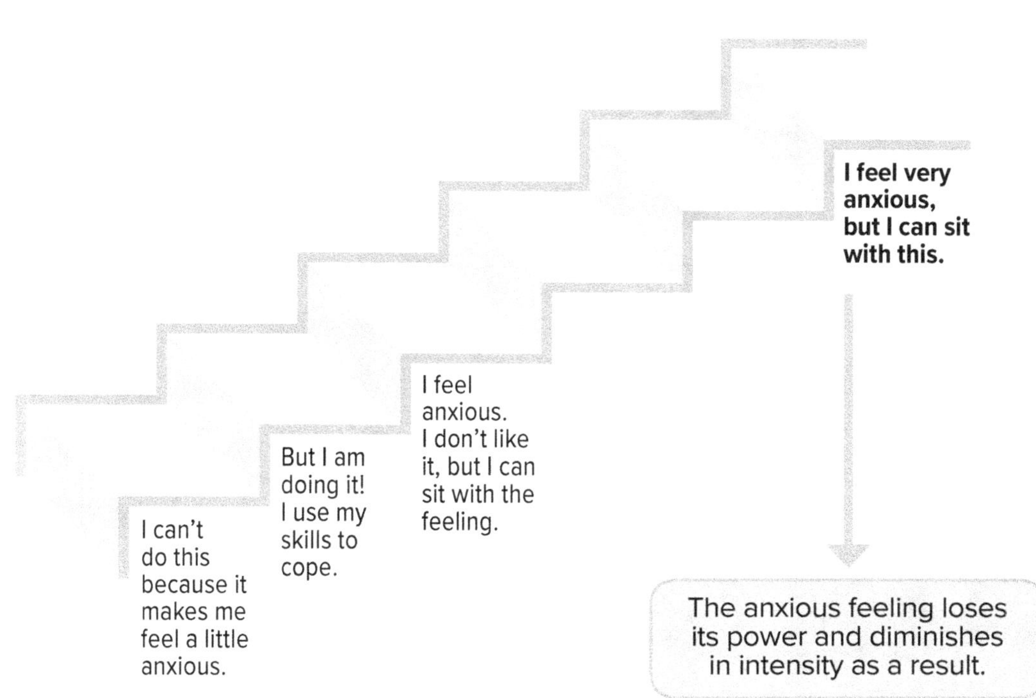

Figure 86

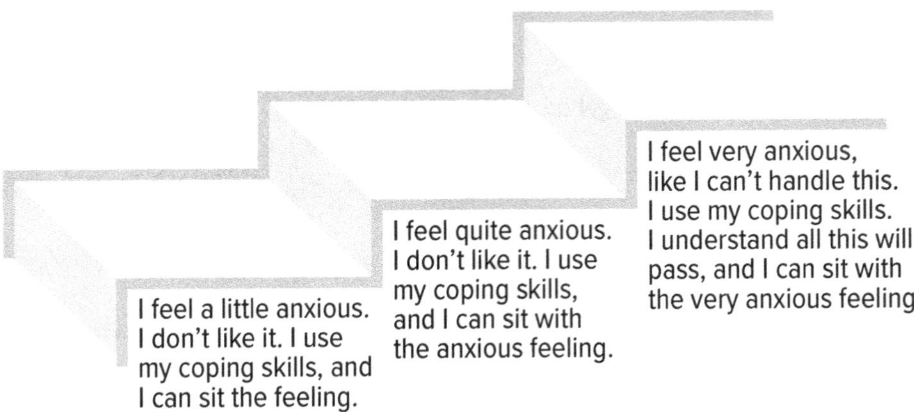

Anxious feelings increase step-by-step. It becomes clear that you can sit
with any anxious feeling. You lose your fear of the anxious feeling.
It loses its power. The anxious part of the feeling diminishes over time.
It's still a feeling. But you no longer avoid it or suffer from it.

Figure 87

The **moderately anxious** feeling I am going to sit with is:

____

The coping skills I am going to use are:

____

I will now: **Just sit with it.**

I will not: Be swept away by the anxious feeling or avoid the
anxious feeling.

Figure 88

> The **very anxious** feeling I am going to sit with is:
>
> ____
>
> The coping skills I am going to use are:
>
> ____
>
> I will now: Just sit with it.
>
> I will not: Be swept away by the anxious feeling or avoid the anxious feeling.

Figure 89

- Thinking about heights
- Talking about heights

- Beginning with low-level exposure (going near a bridge)
- Moving to moderate exposure (taking a step onto a bridge)
- Moving to high-level exposure (crossing a bridge)

- Exposure to trauma elements following the steps outlined above
- Combined with other elements of CBT such as behavioral and cognitive interventions

Figure 90

References

ACEs Science 101. (2018, July 10). Retrieved from https://acestoohigh.com/aces-101/

American Psychiatric Association. (2013). *Diagnostic and statistical manual of mental disorders* (5th ed.). Arlington, VA: Author.

Beck, A. T., Rush, A. J., Shaw, B. F., & Emery, G. (1979). *Cognitive therapy of depression.* New York, NY: Guilford Press.

Bunge, E., Mandil, J., Consoli, A., & Gomar, M. (2017). *CBT strategies for anxious and depressed children and adolescents: A clinician's toolkit.* New York, NY: Guilford Press.

Dimeff, L., & Linehan, M. (2001). Dialectical behavior therapy in a nutshell. *The California Psychologist, 34,* 10-13.

Dobson, D., & Dobson, K. (2017). *Evidence-based practice of cognitive behavioral therapy.* New York, NY: Guilford Press.

Fefergrad, M., & Zaretsky, A. (2013). *Psychotherapy essentials to go: Cognitive behavioral therapy for anxiety.* New York, NY: Norton & Company.

Fisher, J. E., & O'Donohue, W. (2006). *The practitioner's guide to evidence-based psychotherapy.* New York, NY: Springer.

Jong, P. D., & Berg, I. K. (2013). *Interviewing for solutions.* Australia: Brooks/Cole Cengage Learning.

Persons, J. B., Davidson, J., & Tompkins, M. A. (2001). *Essential forms for essential components of cognitive-behavior therapy for depression.* Washington, DC: American Psychological Association.

Society of Clinical Psychology. (2016). *Generalized anxiety disorder.* American Psychological Association. Retrieved from https://www.div12.org/diagnosis/generalized-anxiety-disorder/

Society of Clinical Psychology. (2016). *Panic disorder.* American Psychological Association. Retrieved from https://www.div12.org/diagnosis/panic-disorder/

Society of Clinical Psychology. (2016). *Social phobia and public speaking anxiety.* American Psychological Association. Retrieved from https://www.div12.org/diagnosis/social-phobia-and-public-speaking-anxiety/

Society of Clinical Psychology. (2016). *Specific phobias.* American Psychological Association. Retrieved from https://www.div12.org/diagnosis/specific-phobias/

Schore, J. R., & Schore, A. N. (2008). Modern attachment theory: The central role of affect regulation in development and treatment. *Clinical Social Work Journal, 36,* 9-20. doi: 10.1007/s10615-007-0111-7

Tolin, D. F. (2016). *Doing CBT: A comprehensive guide to working with behaviors, thoughts, and emotions.* New York, NY: Guilford Press.

Wehrenberg, M. (2017). *Tough-to-treat anxiety: Hidden problems and effective solutions for your clients.* New York, NY: Norton & Company.